THE BOOK OF HEROES

Great Men and Women
in American History

THE BOOK OF HEROES

Great Men and Women in American History

George Roche

with Lissa Roche

VOLUME 1

REGNERY PUBLISHING, INC.
Washington, D.C.

Library of Congress Cataloging-in-Publication Data

George Roche.
    Heroes: great men and women in American history / George Roche : with Lissa Roche.
              p.   cm.
    Includes bibliographical references and index.
    ISBN 0-89526-381-5 (alk. paper)
    1. Heroes—United States—Biography. 2. United States—Biography.
    I. Roche, Lissa. II. Title.
    CT214.G46   1998
    920.02—dc21   98-10025
                                                     CIP

Published in the United States by
Regnery Publishing, Inc.
An Eagle Publishing Company
One Massachusetts Avenue, NW
Washington, DC 20001

Distributed to the trade by
National Book Network
4720-A Boston Way
Lanham, MD 20706

Printed on acid-free paper.
Manufactured in the United States of America.

Designed by Kristine Lund.
Set in Sabon.

10 9 8 7 6 5 4 3 2 1

Books are available in quantity for promotional or premium use. Write to Director of Special Sales, Regnery Publishing, Inc., One Massachusetts Avenue, NW, 20001, for information on discounts and terms or call (202) 546-5005.

CONTENTS

FOREWORD

HERO-BASHING HAS BECOME THE NORM for modern
historians and journalists. The vacuum this bashing has
created has been filled not by great men and women who
demonstrate the best qualities of humanity but by antiheroes—
individuals celebrated for their eccentricities and their willingness
to challenge tradition and convention.

As parents, we all desire to live a life worthy of emulation by
our children, but we recognize that our children need heroes outside the family who can inspire them to achieve the kind of out-
ward greatness that comes from sound inner character.

During my school years, I read dozens of biographies of
great Americans. These were distinguished by having been written not only for children, but also for interested adults. I have no
doubt that my early love for the law, education, and public policy was heavily influenced by this pattern of reading.

George Roche's *The Book of Heroes: Great Men and
Women in American History* comes at an opportune time in our
nation's history. More and more, parents are rejecting the amoral
skepticism that has dominated our culture for the past thirty
years, and they are looking for more traditional paths for their
own children.

This book constitutes a path well worth walking with your
children. Read it aloud to the young ones. Pass it on to the older
ones as well as to other family members, college students, teachers,
friends, and business associates. *Heroes* is valuable reading for
anyone who wants to know more about our American heritage.

George Washington is portrayed as a unique actor on the stage of history whose like we may never see again. Daniel Boone's real-life exploits prove to be even more incredible than any "tall tale." Louisa May Alcott's literary genius, nurtured by a desire to sacrifice everything for her family, is nothing less than awe-inspiring. The intelligence, persistence, and creative drive of George Washington Carver and Andrew Carnegie are a monument to American ingenuity and enterprise. And the story of unswerving loyalty and devotion that is evident in the bittersweet life of Robert E. Lee is profoundly moving.

A few of the mistakes these individuals made (that revisionist historians dwell upon almost to the exclusion of anything else) are mentioned in passing, but they are placed in the context of truly great lives. I want my ten children to know that their own occasional errors will not end their opportunities "to do well by doing good." And I am confident that the stories presented here will help them understand that greatness is made possible by striving to do their best and by the kind of strong and enduring faith that these six individuals shared.

MICHAEL P. FARRIS
PRESIDENT
HOME SCHOOL LEGAL DEFENSE ASSOCIATION

ACKNOWLEDGMENTS

MUCH OF THE CREDIT FOR *The Book of Heroes* belongs to my co-author and daughter-in-law, Lissa Roche. Her cheerful and patient assistance at every stage of research, writing, and editing has been invaluable.

There are some original conclusions and new points of emphasis in this volume; its main purpose, however, is to share stories that have been told in the past but that have been forgotten today, thanks to modern-day demythologizers and debunkers. I apologize for any instance in which I appear to be using the work of other authors without due credit; sometimes certain words and ideas have been used so many times in a particular case that they have fallen into a kind of literary public domain. I hope I have been able to avoid appropriating too much.

As to the format: The italicized sections in each chapter are fictionalized, but they do describe real people and events. Punctuation and spelling in some quotations have been modernized. And source footnotes—a great distraction, especially for young readers—are avoided, but the recommended reading at the end of each chapter does list the sources cited. In addition, every effort has been made to reconcile conflicting historical accounts and dates, of which there are many, and to present the facts inasmuch as they can be known.

GEORGE ROCHE

PREFACE

F OR A LONG TIME NOW, friends and associates have been
urging me to write an American history text designed for students as well as interested laymen. Without a doubt, there is an
urgent need for not just one but dozens of books like this.
Recently, in helping to prepare reading lists for Hillsdale College's
model school, the Hillsdale Academy, I discovered firsthand how
scarce good books for young learners are these days. As the father
of four children, I have an even more compelling reason to be
interested in what is available. Three of my children are grown
now, but the fourth is about to begin high school. I also have two
grandsons; one is in college and the other is in diapers. My mission as a parent and as a grandparent is to teach these young men
how they should live. The youngest is barely old enough to walk,
let alone read, but I have already begun to think about what he
should read when the time comes, and I have started a list of my
favorite titles. However, I have not been able to find one special
kind of history, a real-life *Book of Virtues*, about the great
American heroes I admired when I was a youth.

Such a history is especially important in our cynical age
in which the media, the academic elite, and the purveyors of
popular culture seem interested only in debunking heroes and in
portraying our nation's past as a dreary, oppressive contest
between contending interest groups. These demythologizers don't
realize the real meaning, purpose, or power of myth. They automatically assume that every myth is merely an imaginary tale, or
a fantastic legend, or an outright falsehood invented to explain

the unknowable, entertain the masses, or sanitize the biography of a public figure. They fail to realize that there is another kind of myth that embodies the most important truths of human existence and that celebrates the "permanent things" in the history of civilization. This is the myth that instructs and inspires. It is also the highest form of teaching and learning.

For the sake of all the children in this world, we must recover this sense of myth and resurrect our heroes. The good news is that parents everywhere, fed up with our antiheroic culture, are calling for a return to the traditional, time-tested forms of value-laden learning that once served this country so well. As former U.S. Secretary of Education William Bennett has written:

> Attention to good character, to standards of right and wrong, even to the study of heroes, seems to be making a comeback. This is encouraging because heroes elevate not only the individual by dint of inspiration but the larger society as well by reinforcing the ideas and virtues necessary for its continuance. In the *Politics,* Aristotle defined education as that which equipped students to discern the good from its counterfeit and to prefer the former to the latter. Children need to know what deserves to be loved and nurtured, but knowledge of these things is not transmitted by genes; it must be taught. And perhaps the best way to teach it is to offer real-life examples of men and women who have demonstrated the kind of character we think they should possess.

Still, too many heroes remain exiled from the modern classroom. And the stories of those who are studied have been censored or, worse yet, made dry, lifeless, and boring. Educator Diane Ravitch once pointed out that no one was ever tempted to take a basal reader under the covers to be read by flashlight. Our children need exciting and inspiring heroes whose lives pass the "flashlight test." Although fictional heroes are important, they also need heroes they can relate to in their daily lives. These are the heroes they can actually grow up to be, without benefit of superpowers or other literary license.

The stories of six real-life heroes are told in this book—five unforgettable men and one woman whose contributions to American life have lived on long after their passing and whose extraordinary deeds will endure as long as human memory may record. Their lives *resonate* with us; they touch our minds and hearts. They also represent the many facets of the American character as well as a wide variety of backgrounds. They were rich and poor. They were city-bred and country-bred. They were from different races and religions. They represented, in other words, the melting pot that is America.

The melting pot is seldom mentioned any more. We are told by the high priests of Political Correctness that it is just another myth that requires debunking. Only the differences between people—that is to say, their "grievance identities"—matter. However, anyone who impartially examines the lives of George Washington, Daniel Boone, Louisa May Alcott, George Washington Carver, Robert E. Lee, and Andrew Carnegie will discover that the melting pot is not only real but it is also one of the most powerful forces in our national life. It brings us together. It strengthens and sustains us. It is the strongest link between our past, present, and future.

George Washington
Father of Our Country

(1732–1799)

Washington, the brave, the wise, the good.
Supreme in war, in council, and in peace.
Valiant without ambition, discreet without fear,
confident without presumption.
In disaster calm, in success, moderate; in all, himself.
The hero, the patriot, the Christian.
The father of nations, the friend of mankind,
Who, when he had won all, renounced all, and sought
in the bosom of his family and of nature,
retirement, and in the hope of religion, immortality.

—Unknown
Inscription at Mount Vernon

March 1748

    The ground was cold and hard. It felt like a block of ice, even though spring was at hand. The boy tugged the threadbare blanket close around his numbed shoulders and tried to ignore the itchy sensation that crept over his body as the fleas and other vermin that infested it stabbed his rough and reddened skin with a thousand burning pinpricks. It was hours until dawn. The moon wasn't even up yet, and the pitch-black darkness of the forest surrounded the camp in the small clearing like a heavy cloak. He fidgeted while he listened to the other members of the surveying party snoring and scratching in their sleep. Then he began thinking about the trap of twigs and twine he had set before retiring for the night. Would there be a squirrel or perhaps even a rabbit in it by now? Oh, how wonderful it would be to have a hot meal! They had been living on nothing but moldy biscuits and cold jerky for two days. Wild game was plentiful indeed, but they were afraid to fire a shot for fear of letting the Indians know their whereabouts. Finally, he drifted off again, dreaming of the tantalizing aromas he recalled from his mother's kitchen, which was far away over the Blue Ridge Mountains.

    The next morning, the boy was bitterly disappointed; the trap was as empty as his groaning stomach. He sighed, retrieved his twine, stuffed it into a pocket, and began trudging back toward camp to inform the others of the sad news. Suddenly, he heard the low, hoarse gobble of a wild turkey. He froze in his tracks. Perhaps he could catch it. But then there was another call, this one high and trembling, like the sound of a quail. From behind a dozen trees, dark, menacing figures appeared in the early morning mist. The boy gasped. It was an Indian war party, and one of the braves was pointing a musket directly at the heart of the future president of the United States.

GEORGE WASHINGTON DID NOT CUT down a cherry tree with a hatchet and then confess the deed to his father, uttering the memorable line, "I cannot tell a lie." This is simply a legend that has been repeated so many times that it has come to seem true. But it sounds just like something he might have done. And we ought to remember that the real deeds of America's first president were far more amazing than any of the tall tales that have been told about him.

George was born on February 22, 1732, in a small farmhouse along Pope's Creek in Virginia. Sometime after his birth, the family picked up stakes and moved about forty miles away to another humble dwelling at a place that would later be called Mount Vernon. George's father, Augustine Washington, was a justice of the peace, church warden, and sheriff who owned nearly two thousand acres of land. Much of this land was swamp and wilderness. The family was far from wealthy and lived very simply. Even though George's parents could trace their ancestors all the way back to King John, the English sovereign who signed the Magna Carta in 1215, they, like many early American settlers, had to make their own way in the world. The first Washington to set foot on American soil was George's grandfather, John Washington. He was a penniless sailor—and a notorious rogue, if the stories told about him are true—who traded his labor for passage to the "New World" in 1657.

George had two older half-brothers, Lawrence and Augustine, Jr., and an older half-sister, Jane. His mother, Mary Ball Washington, married George's father after his first wife died from illness. Later, George would have younger brothers and sisters: Betty, Samuel, John Augustine, Charles, and Mildred. When he was six, the family moved again, this time to a small tobacco plantation known as Ferry Farm on the banks of the Rappahannock River near Fredericksburg, Virginia. It was here that George would acquire his favorite hobbies—fishing, swimming, shooting, and riding—and he would learn to practice such trades as farming, barrel making, and blacksmithing. He was very practical-minded and curious about how things were made. Although he was a conscientious and hard-working student who received high marks for mathematics and penmanship, he did not find studying easy. He had a reputation among his elders for being uncommonly polite, industrious, honest, and generous-spirited. One of his tutors translated *The Rules of Civility and Decent Behavior in Company and Conversation* (a famous code of conduct devised by French Catholic monks) into English, and George conscientiously wrote down all the rules in his copybook. It was no small task since there were more than a hundred of them. Here are a few examples:

- Speak not when you should hold your peace.
- Let your countenance be pleasant but in serious matters somewhat grave.
- Show not yourself glad at the misfortunes of another though he were your enemy.
- Always submit your judgment to others with modesty.
- Use no reproachful language against anyone....
- Be not hasty to believe flying reports to the disparagement of any.
- Let your conversation be without malice or envy....
- Think before you speak....
- When you speak of God or His attributes, let it be seriously....
- Let your recreations be manful, not sinful.
- Labor to keep alive in your breast that little spark of celestial fire called conscience.

GEORGE DID NOT FORGET THESE RULES or "outgrow them," as so many people do when they finish school. He would attempt to follow them rigorously all his life. He was especially concerned with controlling his temper, which he considered his main weakness. He believed these rules were not just about practicing common courtesy but about developing moral character and moral discipline. They taught moderation, restraint, humility, and charity.[1]

At age fifteen, he completed the rigorous course of study that enabled him to become a professional surveyor. (A surveyor is a kind of explorer and map maker. He measures distances and makes records about the natural features of the land between different geographical points.) A year later, in the spring of 1748, he was invited to accompany a surveying party beyond the Blue Ridge Mountains for his powerful and wealthy neighbor, Lord Fairfax. As the story at the beginning of this chapter reveals, George found hardship and danger in the wilderness. The Indians he encountered along the trail did not attack him or his companions, but they did confiscate supplies and take over the surveying party's camp for about two days. George sat wide-eyed as he watched the braves perform a ritual war dance involving the proud display of a human scalp. Later during the expedition, he was almost burned to death when the straw upon which he was sleeping caught fire. Then he and several others were lost for a time in the vast, trackless forest. He also narrowly avoided being bitten by a rattlesnake.

George loved every moment. The wilderness had a profound impact on him. It tested his mettle and endurance, forced him to improvise to meet unexpected challenges, and opened wide, new vistas in his imagination. He was filled with the restless longing of the pioneer—and if it were not for his family obligations back home in Virginia, he undoubtedly would have become a legendary woodsman and explorer like his contemporary, Daniel Boone.

---

1   Charity was probably the greatest of George's virtues. Friends recalled that throughout his lifetime, no matter how busy or burdened, he "was never lax if anyone knocked on his door to request charity or a loan or advice or actual intervention in tangled affairs."

When he returned from the Fairfax survey, George helped map the acreage at Mount Vernon, the large, undeveloped property along the Potomac River that his half-brother Lawrence inherited. In the next several years, he went on several other frontier treks, gaining valuable experience in woodlore. He also helped lay out the new town of Alexandria and became the official surveyor for Culpeper County, Virginia.

BUT BY THIS TIME, a family crisis had reached a head: Lawrence was desperately ill. He had never fully recovered from a case of tuberculosis contracted during service abroad as an officer in the British army. His physicians recommended immediate removal to a warmer climate in the West Indies. George promptly dropped everything he was doing and abandoned a promising career to help his half-brother make the perilous month-long voyage. It was the only time he would leave his native soil.

They set sail for Barbados in the fall of 1751. A terrible squall blew their ship off course, and they nearly missed the island. When they finally landed, it was right in the middle of an epidemic of smallpox. George caught the disease and might well have died but for his strong constitution. When he finally recovered, he was scarred and weak. In 1752, both Washingtons went home to Virginia. A month after his return, Lawrence died. Eventually, his estate would come into George's possession. Although he was forced to be absent for long periods when his duties as a soldier and president demanded, he would call Mount Vernon home for forty years.

In the meantime, Lawrence's death hit George hard. He was only twenty years old, but already he had lost his father and his half-sister Jane. He could not understand why he now had to lose the half-brother he had long adored as a substitute father and boyhood hero. He was growing more prosperous, but the memory of being "land-rich and cash-poor" haunted him. Lawrence had left behind a mountain of debts, and George felt honor-bound to pay all of them. And, upon his return from Barbados, the young woman he had long courted saw fit to reject his marriage suit. (It was not the last time he would be disappointed in love.) But he was not one to dwell upon his griefs. He pushed them aside and threw himself into his work. Following Lawrence's example, he applied for a military appointment in Virginia's volunteer army commissioned by the Crown. In 1753, at the age of twenty-one, he was given the rank of major.

October 1753

"What we need," Governor Dinwiddie exclaimed, throwing up his hands in exasperation, "is someone who has the right breeding and the right skills but who is not so well bred or so talented that we can't afford to lose him. He must be dependable but expendable. Where in the world are we going to find such a paragon?"

The officer to whom this question was addressed replied, "If I may be so bold, your excellency, I think I know just the fellow, one of the adjutants in the militia. He comes from a respectable but not overly prominent family. He is eager for promotion, and he has considerable frontier experience."

"Are you sure he is the man for the job?" the governor pressed. "We are talking about a journey of a thousand miles, and that's if the Indians or the winter blizzards don't kill him before he can complete his mission. I can assign him a small escort—perhaps half-a-dozen civilians. But it will be his sole responsibility to find the French forces and deliver the Crown's ultimatum: Leave the Ohio Valley or else."

"Or else what?" the officer inquired.

"Or else prepare for war," Dinwiddie said grimly.

George was excited and not a little nervous. Of all the colonial officers serving in the British army, he alone had been chosen as a royal emissary. He knew that he had taken on a dangerous, even foolhardy, assignment, but it was a chance at high adventure, to plunge deep into the uncharted wilderness once more. It would be such fun!

How bitterly he would reflect on these naïve sentiments only a short time later. They set out for the Ohio Valley— the great territory that lay west of the Blue Ridge and Allegheny Mountains—in October of 1753. Early snows made travel on horseback sheer torture, but somehow they made it all the way to Fort LeBoeuf[2] to deliver the notice of eviction to the French army. The officers who received George treated him with undisguised contempt, as did the Indian chiefs in Logtown when he—a mere junior officer with no troops or treaty goods—foolishly tried to remind them of their sworn allegiance to the king of England.

Worse yet, George detected signs that the French and their Indian allies were preparing to invade British settlements along the frontier. There were great quantities of arms and more than two hundred war canoes stockpiled at the fort in readiness for a spring campaign. He and his men had to return home immediately to warn Governor Dinwiddie. But it was December now, and the snowdrifts had piled so high that their horses had foundered. The men wanted to bivouac and wait for better weather, but that would mean a delay of months. George couldn't wait. He and Christopher Gist, the fur trader who had been hired as the party's translator, went on alone and on foot. George didn't like Gist. He was dirty, uncouth, and not much of a translator, despite his boasts. But he was the only logical choice.

---

2 Near present-day Waterford, Pennsylvania, and only a few miles from the shores of Lake Erie.

*When George and Gist, half-frozen and nearly starv-
ing, struggled into a village of the Delaware tribe omi-
nously named Murdering Town, they still had hundreds of
miles to travel. They rested briefly and hired a guide who
promised to show them a shortcut over the mountains.
One morning, not long after this, they rose to find the sun
shining and reflecting brightly on the fresh fallen snow.
The air was calm and almost warm. It was a welcome
relief after days of overcast skies and biting cold. George
and Gist couldn't help grinning, suddenly very much in
charity with one another. Who could be disagreeable on
such a fine day? The only one who didn't seem enthused
was their Indian guide. George wondered what the man
was thinking: His dark, expressionless eyes never seemed
to give anything away.*

*They packed up their ragged blankets and munched
absently on hardtack as they struggled eastward, the guide
in the lead. Perhaps they might make five to ten miles
today, if they were lucky. Suddenly, the guide turned as if
to warn them of some danger ahead. A loud explosion
sounded in George's ears and the acrid smell of burnt gunpowder filled the air. From only a few paces away, the
guide had fired his musket point-blank at them. It took
only a second or two to realize that his shot had missed.
George and Gist ran to overpower him before he could
reload.*

"Let's kill him now!" Gist cried.

*George, who was much bigger and stronger, had to
restrain the angry fur trader from carrying out this grisly
deed. "No. We must not kill him."*

*"But what if he leads his tribe to us? We can't let him
go!"*

*"We'll just have to take the risk. Now, I order you to
release him," George said in his steeliest officer's voice.*

The Indian was clearly confused by this exchange, which was in English, and because his captors appeared to be freeing him. But he decided not to tarry to find out what was going on and fled back down the trail toward Murdering Town. George and Gist departed just as rapidly in the opposite direction.

Gist grumbled and swore nonstop for two days. At least George assumed he did. They split up several times as they traveled toward the banks of the Monongahela River. When they reached the river it was not, as they hoped, frozen solid. They had to build a raft using only knives and a crude hatchet. Before they boarded, George looked at the deep roiling black waters that were moving incredibly swiftly despite the great chunks of ice, stone, and uprooted trees that choked the riverbed. He took a deep breath, jumped on the raft, and pushed off from the shore with a long pole he had fashioned from a sapling. They were off, and it seemed as if the Monongahela would quickly swallow them whole, like the whale that swallowed Jonah. The current carried them for only a few minutes before they hit an ice floe. George dug his pole deep into the river and pushed hard. But the raft didn't budge; instead, he was thrown overboard. The icy water grabbed him, shook him like a rag doll, and drove all the air from his lungs. But before the current could sweep him downstream, he summoned all his strength and grabbed hold of the raft. With Gist's help, he crawled aboard, shivering and miserable. As soon as they could, they abandoned the raft and took refuge on a small island.

Gist was also thoroughly drenched by now. "Just look at us," he said through chattering teeth, "We're pale as ghosts. Even our clothes are white and stiff with ice."

"We'll soon be ghosts if we don't find a way to get off this island! Oh, why did we leave the raft?" George said *with a flash of temper that was instantly regretted. "Look here, I didn't mean to lash out at you. I apologize. Try rubbing your fingers and toes to keep them from freezing, and I'll round up some kindling."*

All through the night, they took turns staying awake, feeding a small fire with what twigs they could find. When the sun rose over the horizon, they were too tired to move or even speak. But, lo and behold, a miracle had occurred! The temperature had dropped so low that the river had frozen again. Why, they could walk to the far shore as easily as promenading down a city street—that is, if their numbed and nearly crippled feet could carry them.

THE TWO MEN FINALLY did make it back to Virginia. As Governor Dinwiddie predicted, they had traveled one thousand miles on their incredible journey. Hoping to arouse public sentiment against French imperial ambitions in the West, the British government rushed George's diary (in which he had faithfully made daily entries) into print and distributed it in London and throughout the colonies. A few months later, after being promoted to the rank of lieutenant colonel, George was sent into the wilderness again. This time, relying on his own judgment instead of the governor's orders, he decided to try to oust the French by force. It was a disastrous mistake. In an incident that would help trigger the French and Indian War, his troops fell into a fight in which they unwittingly killed a French diplomatic envoy.[3] Knowing that the enemy would retaliate in force, George should have beat a hasty retreat back to Virginia, but instead he directed his men to build a small fortification called Fort Necessity. Unfortunately, he picked a site near a creek that was prone to

---

3   The dates for the French and Indian War are 1756–1763, but, as this chapter will reveal, there were a number of battles prior to the official declaration of war.

flooding. And he lacked the manpower to mount an adequate defense. The French attacked during a heavy rain that ruined the fort's gunpowder supplies and soaked the soldiers' muskets. More than one hundred colonials were killed or wounded, and George was forced to surrender. It was a humiliating lesson. He felt that his own inadequacies as a military strategist were to blame for the carnage. But when he arrived home in Virginia, he was actually hailed as a hero for standing up to a superior French force. He forgot all about his shameful performance and foolishly hoped for a promotion. When it didn't come, he resigned his commission.

A year later, George would finally have the chance to redeem himself and to show whether he had learned from his mistakes. He volunteered as an aide to Major General Edward Braddock, a regular army officer fresh from England who commanded a detachment of more than a thousand soldiers. In an ambush attack on the British troops on the road to Fort Duquesne[4] in July of 1755, George displayed the bravery and cool-headedness under fire that would make him a living legend. Though stricken with what was probably dysentery, he mounted a horse and joined in the fight. He tried to convince Braddock to let the colonial militiamen "engage the enemy in their own way" by fighting guerrilla-style, but the older and supposedly wiser man insisted that all his troops maintain straight lines of defense. This made every soldier, including Braddock, an easy target. In fact, the general was one of the early casualties. It was a wonder that George himself wasn't hit. He stayed in the thick of battle even though two mounts were shot out from under him and his hat and uniform were riddled with bullet holes.

When the men on the front line could hold their positions no longer, they began to run pell-mell for the rear. George was one of the officers who stopped them and helped organize an

---

4   The future site of Pittsburgh, Pennsylvania.

orderly retreat. He even made sure that Braddock—whom everyone had abandoned since his wound appeared to be mortal—was carried to safety. Without pause for rest, he and two guides then rode some forty miles to summon reinforcements. In his diary, he recorded that he was so ill by this time that he was "wholly unfit for the execution of the duty....The shocking scenes which presented themselves in this night march are not to be described. The dead, the dying, the groans, the lamentations, and cries along the road of the wounded for help....were enough to pierce a heart of adamant, the gloom and horror of which was not a little increased by the impervious darkness occasioned by the close shade of thick woods." At times, he and the guides actually had to dismount and crawl on their hands and knees to find the trail.

George promptly dropped everything he was doing and abandoned a promising career to help his half-brother.

IN 1755, GEORGE WAS APPOINTED commander of Virginia's colonial troops. He was only twenty-three years old. He had gained the respect and admiration of everyone around him, and this time he genuinely deserved it. He served for three years and then returned to Mount Vernon to become a planter and member of the House of Burgesses, Virginia's colonial assembly. In 1759, he wed a wealthy widow named Martha Custis. Though the couple's friends doubted that theirs was a romantic match, it would prove to be a wonderful and loving marriage. Martha was known for her cheerful, generous disposition. She described herself as "an old-fashioned housekeeper, steady as a clock, busy as a bee, and cheerful as a cricket." George immediately took to her son Jackie and daughter Patsy. (Tragically, both would die prematurely; Patsy at age seventeen in 1773 from epilepsy and Jackie at age twenty-seven from a contagious disease contracted in a Continental Army camp in 1781.)

IN 1763, THE FRENCH AND INDIAN WAR ended, and France was forced to give up its claims on the Ohio Valley. George was relieved; the horrors of that brutal frontier war would haunt him for the rest of his life. He never dreamed he would wear a soldier's uniform again, much less that he would fight against his own countrymen and allies. He spent all his time studying new scientific methods of farming: "He read every book and journal on the subject, and he exchanged letters with experts throughout Europe. He conducted endless experiments....He invented a plow that automatically dropped seeds into furrows. He was his own architect....He conducted time and motion studies a century-and-a-half before 'efficiency experts' introduced the concept into American manufacturing." But trouble was brewing at home and abroad—trouble that would lead George, like thousands of others, to lay down the plow and take up the sword.

IN THE 1760s AND 1770s, Americans protested restrictive new regulations Parliament imposed on the colonies after a long period of "Salutary Neglect" in which they had been allowed to direct their own affairs. The Proclamation of 1763 prohibited western expansion beyond the Appalachian Mountains. The old Navigation Acts dating back to the 1650s were "reinterpreted" to curb colonial commerce. The Stamp Act (1765) required taxes on all printed material, from newspapers and books to marriage licenses and deeds. The Declaratory Act (1766) made colonial legislatures subordinate to the king and Parliament. The Townshend Acts (1767) levied duties on imports of basic goods like tea, ink, glass, and paper. The Quartering Act (1765) forced families to provide free lodging to British troops. This was taxation without representation. It was also a blatant attack on the traditional "rights of Englishmen"—rights colonists had enjoyed for well over a century.

George was so disturbed that in April of 1769 he wrote a letter stating: "At a time when our lordly masters in Great Britain will be satisfied with nothing less than the deprivation of American freedom, it seems highly necessary that something shou'd be done to avert the stroke and maintain the liberty which we have derived from our ancestors...." He did not support the early calls for revolution, but he did agree to serve as a member of the Virginia delegation to the First Continental Congress in 1774. Fifty delegates from the thirteen colonies debated how to respond to British oppression but failed to reach a consensus. The Second Continental Congress met in 1775, after the first shots between the Redcoats and the Minutemen were fired at Lexington and Concord. George attended Congress in his old militia uniform, signaling that he thought the time to raise an army had come at last. John Adams, the Massachusetts delegate, nominated George, the "gentleman from Virginia," as commander-in-chief. His election was unanimous.

George was forced to surrender. It was a humiliating lesson. He felt that his own inadequacies as a military strategist were to blame for the carnage.

Why did Congress choose him? True, George stood well over six feet tall—a huge height in those days when the average was almost a foot shorter—and had a very distinguished bearing. He looked the part of a general all right, but his military experience was no more impressive than that of several other candidates. He had been a member of the Virginia legislature for sixteen years, but he was neither a leading politician nor a great orator. At forty-three, he was young and energetic, but his age also counted against him. Perhaps Congress chose George because he had the right combination of character traits—traits, moreover, he had possessed all his life. He was "a man whom everyone seemed to notice even though he said relatively little." He was quiet yet commanding, confident yet humble, resourceful yet steady, brave yet cautious. Most of all, he was the type of man who never quit, no matter how difficult the odds. If the American cause had to rest on the shoulders of one man, the delegates knew unquestionably that the man had to be George Washington.

George's first challenge as head of the Continental Army was daunting. The colonies had no professional soldiers, only fifteen thousand green volunteers who disliked taking orders and who had no real notion of what was required to face the world's largest and most disciplined fighting machine. The Americans were also underequipped and untrained. For the entire course of the war, George would have trouble trying to remedy the first problem, but he would succeed magnificently when it came to the second. He taught his soldiers to learn from their mistakes, just as he had.

He was not at the famous battle of Bunker (or Breed's) Hill, but in March of 1776, George's first major military action was to drive the British from Boston by placing fifty captured cannons on the heights overlooking the city. He thus won a great victory without a battle, and this gave the colonists hope that their cause would prevail.

ON JULY 4, 1776, the Declaration of Independence was issued. The second paragraph opened with the famous words, "We hold these truths to be self-evident, that all Men are created equal, that they are endowed by their Creator with certain unalienable Rights, that among these are Life, Liberty, and the Pursuit of Happiness—That to secure these rights governments are instituted among Men, deriving their just Powers from the Consent of the Governed...." George took heart from these words. He was now officially leading a fight for freedom. Just two days earlier, on July 2, 1776, he had issued a stirring message on this theme in his general orders to the troops:

> The time is now at hand which must probably determine whether Americans are to be Freemen or Slaves; whether they are to have any property they can call their own; whether their Houses and Farms are to be pillaged and destroyed, and they consigned to a State of Wretchedness from which no human efforts will probably

deliver them. The fate of unborn Millions will now depend, under God, on the Courage and Conduct of this army.... We have therefore to resolve to conquer or die: Our own Country's Honor calls upon us for a vigorous and manly exertion, and if we now shamefully fail, we shall become infamous to the whole world. Let us therefore rely upon the goodness of the Cause, and the aid of the supreme Being, in whose hands Victory is, to animate and encourage us to great and noble Actions—The Eyes of all our Countrymen are now upon us, and we shall have their blessings and praises, if happily we are the instruments of saving them from the Tyranny meditated against them. Let us therefore animate and encourage each other and show the whole world that a Freeman contending for Liberty on his own ground is superior to any slavish mercenary on earth.

King George and Parliament scoffed at such talk. They were supremely confident that the soldiers they had sent to quash the rebellion would do so quickly and easily. In July of 1776, twenty thousand of them were led by the British commander-in-chief General Howe in an invasion of New York. George, with only nine thousand defenders, was outmanned and outgunned. At the ensuing Battle of Brooklyn Heights, his army suffered fifteen hundred casualties. To George's dismay, his troops broke ranks and ran away from the British in confusion and panic. Luckily, General Howe did not press his advantage right away. He waited several days to launch a final attack in which total victory for the royal cause seemed assured. In the interim, George played a trick that surely must have been recalled from his youth at Ferry Farm. He rounded up a fleet of rowboats and barges and ferried his entire army across the East River in the middle of the night. When the British commander woke up one morning, it was to find that the Americans had vanished!

In the next few months, the British won most of the battles that were fought. So many American soldiers were killed, injured, or lost through desertion or the expiration of their enlistment that the Continental Army could field only about seven thousand men. By December of 1776, the situation seemed nearly hopeless, especially since the current militia enlistment was due to expire on January 1. Then the British made things even worse by offering pardons to all rebels. Many took them because they believed the American cause was lost. "Now," observed one of his biographers, "was the time for Washington's genius to flourish, if he could summon it." And he did. First, he persuaded his militiamen to extend their enlistment. One soldier remembers him pleading, "My brave fellows, you have done all that I have asked you to do, and more than can be reasonably expected....You have worn yourselves out with fatigue and hardships, but we know not how to spare you. If you will consent to stay only one month longer, you will render service to the cause of liberty and to your country which you can probably never do under any other circumstances."

He then planned a bold surprise attack on the Hessian mercenary troops at Trenton, New Jersey. On Christmas night, twenty-four hundred Continental soldiers (some without coats or shoes) marched nine miles through hail and snow to the Delaware River. As in New York, they ferried across, but in the process most of their gunpowder and muskets were soaked. Conditions were so difficult that two divisions were turned back; only the one under George's command made it successfully. Still, he chose to press the attack—and captured nearly one thousand soldiers and a huge ammunitions store. It was a victory that the Americans desperately needed, and it was quickly followed by another in January of 1777 at Princeton. After a twenty-mile night march, George led his men to within thirty yards of the enemy. This time, it was the British, not the Americans, who broke ranks and ran.

December 1777
It had been a very bad year. Since Trenton and Princeton, he had not been able to mount a serious offen-

sive against the British; indeed, his only objective had been keeping his ragged army alive. In September, his efforts to defend Philadelphia at the Battle of Brandywine not only failed miserably but cost nearly eight hundred casualties. In October, the surprise attack he had carefully planned at Germantown backfired due to bad weather, and he had nearly been relieved of his command, thanks to a political conspiracy among some of his officers who charged him with being incompetent. But there had also been one great shining victory that fall: Saratoga. George nearly let out a whoop when the courier arrived from New York with the news that Generals Gates and Arnold had captured General Burgoyne and five thousand British soldiers.⁵ But he merely smiled and asked the courier to send both gentlemen his compliments.

Meanwhile, just eighteen miles away in Philadelphia— less than a day's march—General Howe was no doubt sitting before a blazing fire consuming a sumptuous feast. How he would laugh if he knew that George was stuck in a drafty log hut with only a poor bowl of stew consisting of boiled turnips and potatoes.

His aide seemed to sense what he was thinking and said piteously, "I'm sorry, General Washington. I searched the quartermaster's wagons, but there wasn't any beef to be had, and what vegetables I could find were mostly rotten. Won't you reconsider moving into one of the nearby villages? You would be much more comfortable, and the food would be a darned sight better."

---

5   General Horatio Gates was commander of the northern army and received most of the credit for the victory at Saratoga, but it was really General Benedict Arnold who was responsible for the outcome. He was a hero of the American Revolution until he secretly changed sides and joined the British cause in 1780. George was devastated by the betrayal of this brilliant military strategist and close personal friend.

"*Not while my men are still living in tents,*" George vowed firmly. "*I intend to remain here until every last soldier has a roof over his head. You know what old Ben Franklin says, don't you? 'A good example is the best sermon.' If the men know that I am willing to endure these frightful conditions, they will be willing to do the same. Now, would you be so kind as to fetch some paper? I think I will write another letter to Congress before I retire for the evening.*"

"*Another request for provisions? But you have written so many such letters, General. I doubt that anyone reads them.*"

"*That doesn't excuse me from my duty to write them,*" George reminded the man gently. Holding a quill pen between stiff, aching fingers and squinting to see in the dim, flickering candlelight, he began to write: "*There are now in this army four thousand men wanting blankets, near two thousand of them have never had one, altho' some of them have been twelve months in service.*" The words were wrung from his heart as he tried once more to describe the wretchedness and suffering in camp. The scrawny, young boys with gray, pinched faces like old men. The ones without coats, stockings, or shoes. The ones who could not drill because they were weak from malnutrition. And the ones with deep, racking coughs like Lawrence. A vivid image of his half-brother leapt to mind and forced George to stop and rub his eyes in order to hold back the tears. A moment later, he shook off his anguish and picked up the quill again: "*Naked and starving as they are, we cannot enough admire the incomparable patience and fidelity of soldiery.*" He affixed his signature and underneath it wrote the two words that in his mind would be forever linked with pain: Valley Forge.

THE LETTER WAS READ, but the only word that came back from Congress was this: Since the local tradesmen and farmers would not accept Continental currency (the paper money Congress issued that was practically worthless), George was advised to confiscate what he needed, at gunpoint if necessary. He refused, pointing out that it was this kind of abuse of power that had led the colonists to revolt in the first place. Finally, by mid-February of 1778, Congress sent just enough supplies for the army to survive the rest of the winter. The soldiers also finished building their huts, so George agreed to make a modest farmhouse his new headquarters.

He was right to insist that his moral example could inspire others. The soldiers did not desert at Valley Forge. This was not because they were storybook heroes who were indifferent to cold, hunger, or pain. They were common folk, mostly just a bunch of semiliterate farmers and tradesmen who despised Congress for abandoning them and who were terrified of facing the most fearsome army in the world. They stayed because they had faith in one man: George Washington. Of course, George did not gain their loyalty and devotion overnight. He earned it gradually over many years in a hundred incidents that revealed

In 1755, George was appointed commander of Virginia's colonial troops. He was only twenty-three years old. He had gained the respect and admiration of everyone around him.

the true depth of his character. During a night march in the French and Indian War, for example, he undertook to stop soldiers who were accidentally shooting one another in the dark. One account describes the scene memorably: "[H]e stepped between their blazing muskets and struck them up with his sword." In a number of fierce contests during the American Revolution, he stood his ground while the raw recruits around him panicked and ran. When he accepted his commission as commander-in-chief of the Continental Army, he refused the handsome salary offered by Congress, asking only to be reimbursed for his expenses. He also refused to leave his troops except for the briefest periods and went home to visit Mount Vernon on only two occasions during the entire war.[6]

As spring approached in Valley Forge, George enlisted a stern Prussian drillmaster to help train the troops and teach them how to fight like the professionals they would be facing in the coming campaign. Also in the spring, word came that France had signed a treaty with the new United States. The news buoyed George's spirits. He had become quite close to a number of young French volunteers in the Continental Army like the Marquis de Lafayette. Now, he hoped he could also count on seasoned French regulars. But the French proved reluctant to risk much of their prestige, manpower, or treasury on such an uncertain cause. So, the war dragged on. The years 1779 and 1780 saw little military action, but they brought paralyzing blizzards in some of the coldest winters on record, as well as more hunger and privation. When even the most honest soldiers began looting and foraging, George reluctantly realized that he would have to demand that civilians accept Continental currency for requisitions. But in the spring of 1780, Connecticut soldiers who had been without meat for ten days mutinied. No one in the army had been paid for five months. Then, in January of 1781, troops in Pennsylvania and New Jersey also mutinied. The Continental Army was on the verge of collapse.

In the fall, however, there was a single ray of hope; George learned that the French fleet was sailing from the West Indies to institute a blockade against General Cornwallis's troops at Yorktown, Virginia. It was a perfect opportunity to spring a trap through a combined land and sea maneuver. First, he had to fool the British commander-in-chief who had replaced Howe, General

---

6   What examples inspired George? From his early schooling and the plays that were popular in his youth, he learned about such heroes of classical antiquity as Cato the Younger (95–46 B.C.), who represented the ancient Roman concepts of virtue, courage, duty, and piety. He also admired the biblical heroes of the Old and New Testaments.

Clinton, into thinking that the Continental Army would attack New York. He arranged for one of his assistants to fall into British hands and make a false confession. He also ordered the erection of a large camp outside the city. A small group of soldiers was charged with keeping campfires burning, baking bread in ovens, and marching about at all hours to make sure the deception was totally convincing. George and the rest of his men then joined French troops and warships to lay siege to the British encampment on the Yorktown peninsula. After eight days, on October 19, 1781, General Cornwallis sent a representative to George's headquarters to surrender his sword. More than eight thousand Redcoats stacked their arms while their military band played a tune called, appropriately enough, "The World Turned Upside Down."

Yorktown was a stunning victory. Although there would be other skirmishes, the War for Independence was essentially won, and the American colonies were free at last. George had made the war unwinnable for the British through a brilliant combination of daring and caution. Unlike the typical eighteenth-century military leader, he wasted nothing and demanded that his men follow his example. He studied the terrain and readily adapted his tactics to a constantly changing set of conditions. He kept his army in the field, but, when he could help it, he committed it to battle only when the odds were overwhelmingly in his favor. And he took full advantage of the fact that the British were reluctant to risk major casualties because replacements had to come at great expense from overseas. When he was appointed commander-in-chief of the Continental Army, George's greatest fear was that if the war were lost, he would be to blame. Now that the war was won, however, he was due a great deal of the credit. But he did not leap to accept it. One historian says:

[He] never regarded fighting the enemy as the fundamental means by which the Revolutionary War would be won. He demonstrated again and again his conviction that the crucial battlefields were in the minds of individual Americans. If the majority decided that they would be better off under the Crown, all military efforts to defeat the British would be of as little avail as trying to stop a river that was perpetually flowing. But, if the people became such staunch supporters of American rights that they would hold steadfast through any emergency, the British might just as well march their military might into the ocean.

George himself would write that the colonies' secret weapon was the "unconquerable resolution" of its citizens.

October 1781

Six years. Six long and desperate years, and now it was all but over. He could return home in triumph. Mount Vernon had suffered terribly from neglect during his absence. He would have his hands full just getting things in order again. But it would be a simple feat compared to the conjurer's trick he had just pulled off at Yorktown. He wondered idly where he had stored his notes on the fertilization experiments he had begun before assuming command of the army. Martha would probably remember. Dear Martha! He felt a surge of joy as he recalled the cheers of the men when they realized that they, too, could finally return to their homes and families. They knew as well as he did, of course, that the army could not be disbanded immediately. It might be months before a treaty could be signed. But they were confident that the members of Congress would finally see fit to award them, without further delay, their back pay and overdue bonuses.

March 1783

He sat with his head in his hands, more discouraged than at any time he could remember. They had been marooned in a dirty, crowded camp in Newburgh, New York, for what seemed like forever. In yet another letter to Congress, he had written that his men were

> *soured by penury and what they call the ingratitude of the public, involved in debts, without one farthing of money to carry them home, after having spent the flowers of their days, and many of them their patrimonies, in establishing the freedom and independence of this country and suffering everything human nature is capable of enduring on this side of death.*

But Congress had once again turned a deaf ear to his pleas. The men had not been paid for months and some had not been paid since their original enlistment! There had been no word about when they would be paid or when they would be discharged. And it wasn't only the enlisted men who were grumbling about this shameful ill-treatment. Just that morning, a frightened lieutenant had shown him another one of the anonymous pamphlets that had been circulating among the officers calling for "immediate measures." George knew there had also been several secret meetings recently. It was only a matter of time before mutiny spread like wildfire through the ranks. The Continental Army had won the war, but now it stood to lose the peace, even before peace was officially declared. With sudden decision, George stood up from his chair and called impatiently for his best uniform. He had to deter his near-mutinous officers.

"I tell you, we can't wait any longer!" said the officer with the black scowl on his face. "Those fools in Philadelphia have dragged their feet for more than a year now. We have to seek justice in our own way."

Another officer, who didn't look any happier, said, "I hate to admit it, but Edward's right. If we don't put the threat of force behind our demands, Congress will think we are bluffing."

"But we could all be hanged!" a third officer objected.

"We will put it to a vote," the first officer announced firmly. "All in favor—" He stopped suddenly and peered through the smoky haze that filled the crowded tavern to inquire suspiciously, "Here now, who is that at the door?"

"Please pardon my abominable tardiness," George said mildly as he flicked an invisible speck of lint from his immaculate uniform. "May I please inquire of the chair, are all those present at this distinguished gathering permitted to speak?"

A chorus of angry voices protested, but the loudest demanded, "Let him speak!"

"It seems that you have the floor, General Washington," the first officer reluctantly conceded.

Suddenly, the room quieted. George could hear his own leather boots creaking as he walked through the sea of officers. They readily parted to make way for him. Their crimson faces revealed embarrassment but also defiance. He doubted that they could be swayed from their dire purpose, but he began to speak anyway. He asked them to be patient just a little while longer. He reminded them that the army could not be a law unto itself. He also pointed out that they had fought together to institute democracy, not a new kind of tyranny. He concluded by saying, "I have a letter here from a congressman that will prove the good faith of our government."

He drew the parchment from his pocket and unfolded it. But the light in the tavern was too dim for him to make out the words. With a trembling hand, he fumbled for his glasses. He hated them and had never worn them in public before. In a deeply mortified tone, he apologized, "Gentlemen, you will permit me to put on my spectacles,

*for I have not only grown gray, but almost blind, in the
service of my country." He started to read the letter, but he
couldn't speak. His voice, as well as his composure,
deserted him. He stalked out of the room without uttering
another word.*

NOW, THE CONTINENTAL ARMY officers were all hardened soldiers who had witnessed terrible sights without flinching. But seeing their beloved commander reduced to such a state, they began
to weep openly. At the tavern meeting at Newburgh on March
15, 1873—which George himself had called but had shrewdly led
the officers to believe he would not attend—they unanimously
pledged to follow orders and quell all attempts at mutiny. Once
again, George had saved the nation from destruction. If the officers had rebelled as they planned, America would have been
plunged into a bloody civil war.

When the troops were finally sent home after the Treaty of
Paris had been signed in the fall of 1783—two years after the
British surrender at Yorktown—George resigned his commission
and returned to Mount Vernon. After nine years of service, not
only his eyesight but his hearing was also impaired. Most of his
teeth had been pulled. Eventually, he would be forced to wear
uncomfortable dentures made of exotic materials like hippopota-
mus ivory.[7] But he was still strong enough to "crack open hard-
shelled nuts with his fingers and even bend a horseshoe with his
bare hands." Even though people turned out to cheer him everywhere he went and he received congratulatory letters from digni-
taries around the world, George humbly assumed that his name
would soon fade into obscurity. He was fully aware that the nation

---

[7]   Legend has it that he wore wooden teeth, but George's dentures were
actually made from a combination of cow teeth, human teeth, and hip-
popotamus ivory.

was still in its infancy and therefore vulnerable, but he hoped others would step forward to assume the mantle of protector.

None did, however. Congress was bankrupt. There was no treasury to pay off the enormous war debt. There was no sound currency. There was no real unity between the former colonies; in its earliest days "the United States was not one nation but thirteen." Unfortunately, the Articles of Confederation, drafted in 1771 and finally ratified in 1781, were not strong enough to solve any but the most minor problems. Then, in late 1786, a mob of poor farmers vainly tried to prevent tax foreclosures on their property by seizing a military arsenal filled with thousands of weapons. Known as Shays's Rebellion, this act shocked the nation and led George to agree to preside over the Constitutional Convention in Philadelphia in 1787. He had no love for tax collectors. On the contrary, he was deeply sympathetic toward the farmers' plight. But he could not condone lawlessness. He had risked his life during the Revolution; now he was risking his reputation, for the meetings in Philadelphia were widely condemned as a secret plot to institute a monarchy or, at the least, to rob the states of their authority. With extraordinary perception he realized "that what was at issue was the grand question of whether a people could govern themselves by a reasonable process of deliberation rather than by the violent force of arms to which every other government on earth owed its origins. In a sense, the Constitutional Convention would be legislating for all mankind."

In the end, George's gamble paid off. The U.S. Constitution was written. It was ratified by the required number of states—nine—in 1788.[8] The promise of independence was finally fulfilled. The new nation would have a limited but effective central government. It would operate through a system of checks and balances invested in three separate branches: executive, legislative, and judicial. Most notably, the head of the executive branch

---

8   In 1791, ten amendments known as the Bill of Rights were added.

would be the president of the United States. What model did the delegates have in mind when they created the office? George Washington, of course.

George was advised to confiscate what he needed, at gunpoint if necessary. He refused, pointing out that it was this kind of abuse of power that had led the colonists to revolt in the first place.

IT WAS NO SURPRISE in 1789 when the electoral college (a voting body established by the Constitution and made up of representatives from every state) unanimously elected George president. But he was deeply distressed. When he resigned from the army, he had pledged to retire from public life. He knew Martha desperately wanted him to remain at home, too. Besides, he reflected somberly, being the first president of a new nation was tantamount to "entering upon an unexplored field, enveloped on every side with clouds and darkness." He felt like a condemned man being sent to the gallows, but duty could not be denied. With an aching in his heart, he bade farewell to Mount Vernon once more.

Wearing a simple suit of brown broadcloth, he was sworn into office in the temporary capital of New York on April 30, 1789. One historian reports: "His left hand rested on the Bible, which had been opened between the 49th and 50th chapters of Genesis. He then kissed the Bible and reverently said, 'So help me God.'" George started another tradition by making an inaugural address to both houses of Congress in which he declared that "the foundation of our national policy [must] be laid in the pure and immutable principles of private morality...there is no truth more thoroughly established than that there exists...an indissoluble union between virtue and happiness...." He added that "the preservation of the sacred fire of liberty and the destiny of the republican model of government are justly considered as deeply, perhaps as finally, staked on the experiment intrusted to the hands of the American people."

George refused to be called "his highness" or "your majesty," as was suggested by those who helped design the new presidential office. He also refused to live like the members of European aristocracy who spent most of their time in pursuit of idle pleasure. Instead, he traveled about the country tirelessly promoting commerce and industry and explaining the workings of the Constitution and the new federal government to ordinary citizens. He did not travel with a grand retinue, and he usually lodged in small country inns without any advance warning. He hated people to make a fuss over him (which they inevitably did), but he found a deep satisfaction in what was primarily an educational rather than a political mission. He was not trained as a scholar and was one of only two presidents who did not earn a college degree, but he maintained a strong interest in ideas, subscribing to ten newspapers and keeping up an active correspondence about the important intellectual issues of the day. Above all, George was keenly aware that forming "a new government requires infinite care," and that his actions as president would establish important precedents. In a letter written near the end of the war, he acknowledged that "we have a national character to establish" and added that it should rest "on permanent principles." The two principles he specifically named were justice and gratitude.

His own dedication to these principles would be severely tested during his eight years as America's first chief executive. There were so many crises in the 1790s: the massive Revolutionary War debt; corruption, ambition, and political intrigue in the federal government and among the states; the weakness of the army (reduced to fewer than seven hundred soldiers); the lack of a navy; Britain's refusal to abandon forts along the northwestern frontier and its persistent efforts to incite Indian attacks against the United States; Spanish territorial ambitions in the southwest; the Whiskey Rebellion led by tax dodgers in western Pennsylvania who not only committed wanton acts of violence but also demanded secession from the Union; the growing gap between southern agrarian and northern commercial interests; the prospect of being drawn into war with Britain, France, or both. And these were just the crises that threatened the nation; George was personally threatened by another series of crises, including a tumor that had to be surgically removed; near-fatal bouts with pneumonia and influenza, a fall from a horse that left him nearly crippled, the death of his favorite nephew from the same dread disease that had killed his half-brother Lawrence, and a ruthless smear campaign conducted by some of his supposed friends to discredit policies they opposed. Fortunately, George knew how to draw upon the lessons of experience as well as his principles in facing all these crises. He was not able, of course, to solve every one and he frequently made mistakes, but he was the most successful president in American history. Here is a brief list of his accomplishments:

→ He examined problems from every side and was not afraid to ask questions. Yet he was prudent and slow to make important decisions or to speak out on public matters because he knew that "his commitments carried more clout than anyone else's on the continent."

→ He earnestly believed in the separation of powers, so only with rare exceptions did he try to propose or influence legislation. He used the presidential veto to protect the Constitution, not to interfere with legislative decisions, no matter how much he disagreed with them. But he was no mere figurehead; he maintained an active and vital role in determining the workings of the new federal government.

→ As a planter, he had gotten deep into debt to the "factors" (middlemen in today's vocabulary) in England who did not offer a fair exchange for his tobacco shipments.

He figured out how to diversify his crops, sell them domestically, and get out of debt. Thereafter, he was his own accountant and investment manager. As president, he applied his considerable business acumen to the nation's finances, calling for full repayment of the Revolutionary War debt plus interest, frugal spending, a balanced budget, and low taxes.

➤ He personally supervised the hiring of nearly one thousand government employees by going against every precedent and custom and judging the merit of the applicants' qualifications instead of their family connections and social status. He also refused to endorse political candidates for fear of giving anyone an unfair advantage.

➤ He defended the freedom of the press, even though he was angered and wounded by frequently scurrilous attacks on his person and his administration.

➤ He advocated a simple code of legal justice that the common man could understand. He undertook the task of educating literally thousands of citizens about the Constitution that was the new law of the land.

➤ He was ahead of his time when it came to defending civil rights. He sought equal treatment for Indians on a par with whites in the courts. He insisted that old and unfair treaties be scrapped. He believed the eastern tribes deserved generous compensation for the sale of their lands and, in cases where fraud was proved, the actual return of lands.[9]

---

[9] George's efforts to establish peace with the eastern tribes failed, however, and in August of 1794 the famous Battle of Fallen Timbers ended in a decisive victory for the United States.

➤ As a Christian, he regarded religion and morality as the "twin pillars" of the free society. His diaries and letters are filled with references to his strong personal faith. He also defended religious freedom and tolerance for such traditionally persecuted groups as the Baptists, Roman Catholics, Quakers, and Jews.

➤ He exhibited personal heroism and profound moral leadership. In the summer of 1793, there was an outbreak of yellow fever in Philadelphia that would prove to be "the most murderous epidemic in American history." Yet he and Martha refused to leave the capital although nearly every other member of the government fled.

➤ He was a peacemaker. When two rival political parties formed, he made sure that he had representatives of both in his cabinet. Avoiding bitter factionalism was one of his strongest concerns. He constantly wrote letters to quarreling politicians in which he recited the virtues of trust, patience, and forgiveness. He also tried to reconcile Yankee businessmen and southern planters. He saw more clearly than anyone else that agrarian and commercial interests must be reconciled if the nation was to survive.

➤ He was a war hero who hated war. He harbored no romantic illusions about soldiering. Therefore, he established a foreign policy based on strict neutrality and, despite considerable pressures, kept his administration free from "entangling alliances" with other nations.

GEORGE LONGED TO RETIRE from the presidency at the end of his first term in 1793, but the Federalists and Democratic–Republicans agreed that he was the only man who "stood above partisan politics; he alone could work with both sides."[10] Thomas Jefferson declared, "North and South will hang together, if they have you to hang on." George was elected unanimously for a second time.[11] Despite all entreaties, however, he refused a third term, observing to one correspondent, "I had rather be at Mount Vernon with a friend or two about me than to be attended at the seat of government by the officers of state and the representatives of every power of Europe." His resignation was an extraordinary historical event. That a ruler would voluntarily hand over the reins of government to another was almost unthinkable; it had rarely ever happened in all human history. By giving his awesome political power back to the people who had entrusted it to him, George gained something far greater than any king ever possessed: He became the father, not just of a country but of the greatest experiment in freedom the world has ever known.

Back at Mount Vernon in the spring of 1797 after an eight-year absence, George said he felt like a weary traveler who had finally come to rest at the inn at the end of the road. But he had one last difficult duty to perform. It began as a matter of personal honor and conscience, but, like so many duties he sought to fulfill, it ended up having a dramatic impact on America. He had gradually come to hate slavery not only because he thought it was immoral and unjust but because he thought it was an evil that corrupted all who tolerated it. He did not believe, as so many people did at the time, that one race had the right to enslave another or that blacks were inferior. During the Revolution, he fought for the desegregation of the Continental

---

10 The Federalist Party was led by Alexander Hamilton and was pro-British. Its rival, which was eventually referred to as the Democratic–Republican Party, was led by Thomas Jefferson and was pro-French. There were other important issues that divided them, but it was their stance on foreign affairs that caused the most dissension.

11 No other president in American history has been elected unanimously; George achieved this feat not once but twice.

Army. In his private correspondence after the war, he supported emancipation. He even told an acquaintance, "I clearly foresee that nothing but the rooting out of slavery can perpetuate the existence of our union," and he concluded by pledging that if the North and South were ever separated over the issue, he would abandon his home and move to the North.

But George Washington was also a slave owner. He had inherited slaves from his father and gained even more when he had married Martha. When he was young, he did not question the institution of slavery, and he benefited from it financially. Even after he came to support emancipation, he did not set more than a few slaves free.[12] He feared his action would ignite a disastrous slave revolt and create unprecedented political turmoil in the South. He also suspected with some justification that his freed slaves would be re-enslaved or would starve because they could not earn a living. Freedom just didn't seem worth the risk. So, George eased his troubled conscience by refusing to break up slave families or to sell a single slave, no matter how many new mouths there were to feed. He was true to his word for more than three decades, even though it cost his estate dearly. When he was elected president, he also supported Secretary of the Treasury Alexander Hamilton's plans for encouraging industry and finance because he privately believed that they would make slavery increasingly uneconomical.

As an old man, his doubts nagged at him: What if freedom was worth the risk? George finally realized that it was. In July of 1799, he wrote a new will ordering that the slaves at Mount Vernon be freed once he and Martha had passed away.[13] The young would be given funds for education. Virginia law prohibited

---

12 When he retired from the presidency and returned to Virginia, George secretly left a few of his household slaves in Pennsylvania where, according to that state's laws, they would be free men and women.

13 Martha's slaves were part of an "entailed" inheritance, which meant that only she could legally free them.

teaching slaves to read and write, but George insisted on this pro-
vision. The old and infirm would be given pensions. Martha knew
all about the terms of his will and she approved so much that she
freed every slave on the estate less than a year after his death.

December 1799

*He rose before dawn and would have been out of the
house before anyone else stirred, but his secretary, Lear, had
left a great pile of correspondence on the desk that needed
sorting. Sometimes he wished he hadn't promised himself that
he would answer every letter he received! He didn't get out to
the stables until about ten o'clock. He loved riding about the
Virginia countryside in the morning hours. The woods,
although not as thick as they once were, reminded him of the
forests in the Ohio Valley. Oh, to tramp the wild places
again! He patted his mount's neck and reined him toward the
outer boundary of the estate. There was a new field he
wanted to inspect before deciding what to grow when the
planting season arrived. He had been out of office for nearly
three years now, but he never ran out of chores to help bring
the land back to its former glory. A freezing rain began to fall
when he reached the field, but he paid it no heed as he dug
up a handful of earth and sifted it through his hands to see if
there was clay mixed with the sod. Perhaps he would plant
wheat. It grew better in clay than most other crops.*

*When he started for home in the late afternoon, the
rain was still falling. He made a mental note to find
Martha a special present when he was next in town.
Christmas was just around the corner. Jackie's children and
all his various nieces and nephews ought to be surprised
with some treats, too, even though they were quite grown
up now. His throat began to ache slightly. He must have
caught a chill. He would rest a bit when he got home.*

"I don't believe it!" Martha scolded him later that evening as she hustled him off to change his clothes. "You ought to know better than to gallivant around the countryside in the dead of winter like a careless young scamp."

"Yes, my dearest," George said meekly. He knew by the little gleam in her eye that his wife was not truly angry with him. But he refused to allow her to call a doctor. "You know I never take anything for a cold. Let it go as it came."

But the cold turned into a raging fever, and then a suffocating cough. He offered no argument when Martha insisted on help this time, but the doctor and the other medical experts called in to assist could offer no remedy. Two days after his fateful ride in the rain, George called for his secretary and inquired if all his outstanding bills were paid.

"Why, yes, your debts are cleared," Lear informed him.

"Then I am quite content. But I have one final debt to pay—the debt we are all obligated to pay to our Maker." Though very weak by now, George still had enough energy to bestow one of his rare smiles on the man. He also begged Lear to tell the doctors not to "take any more trouble" about him. Sometime before midnight, he uttered his final words, "'Tis well."

GEORGE LIVED TO BE SIXTY-SEVEN years old. He died on December 14, 1799. One of his last requests was to be buried "in a private manner without parade or funeral oration" at Mount Vernon. But memorial services were held in virtually every city and town in America. At one ceremony in Philadelphia, more than ten thousand people watched in silence as a white horse bearing his saddle and boots paraded by. Henry Lee, governor of Virginia and a Revolutionary War general, said that George

Washington was "first in war, first in peace, and first in the hearts of his countrymen." Thomas Jefferson, the third president of the United States, was even more laudatory:

> He was incapable of fear, meeting personal dangers with the calmest unconcern. Perhaps the strongest feature in his character was prudence, never acting until every circumstance, every consideration, was maturely weighed; refraining if he saw a doubt, but, when once decided, going through with his purpose, whatever obstacles opposed. His integrity was most pure, his justice the most flexible I have ever known, no motive of interest or consanguinity, or friendship, or hatred, being able to bias his decision. He was, in every sense of the word, a wise, a good, and a great man.

But it was John Adams, the second president of the United States, who predicted that George's legacy would endure forever: "For his fellow citizens, if their prayers could have been answered he would have been immortal....His example is now complete, and it will teach wisdom and virtue to magistrates, citizens, and men, not only in the present age, but in future generations as long as our history shall be read."

George bitterly regretted that he had no children of his own. But since he was the "father of our country," we are all rightly his heirs. He has also been called the "indispensable man." Without him, we might not have won our independence. Without him, our republic might not have survived. Without him, the Constitution and Bill of Rights might not have been written. George showed us the tremendous power of one individual. He created not only a model for the chief executive but also a model for every citizen. He was the living embodiment of what it means to be an American. There will never be another George Washington, but we should all aspire to be like him.

SUGGESTED READINGS

There is a veritable treasure trove of scholarship on George Washington awaiting those who are willing to search for it in library stacks and bookstore basements. Among my favorite books for older readers are James Thomas Flexner's *Washington: The Indispensable Man* [1969] (Little, Brown and Co., 1974) and two titles by Forrest McDonald, *The Presidency of George Washington* (University Press of Kansas, 1974) and *The American Presidency: An Intellectual History* (University Press of Kansas, 1994). McDonald's brief article, "Today's Indispensable Man," in *Modern Age* (Intercollegiate Studies Institute, Spring 1995) is also well worth reading. For younger readers there is Roger Bruns' brief, illustrated biography, *George Washington* (Chelsea House Publishers, 1987). Other sources consulted for this chapter were: Ralph K. Andrist, *George Washington: A Biography in His Own Words* (Newsweek Book Division, 1972); Donald Jackson, *The Diaries of George Washington* (University of Virginia, 1976); Edmund S. Morgan, *The Genius of George Washington* (W. W. Norton & Co., 1980); W.B. Allen, *George Washington: A Collection* (LibertyClassics, 1988); Rosemarie Zagarri, Ed., David Humphrey's *Life of General Washington* (University of Georgia, 1991); Thomas A. Lewis, *For King and Country: The Maturing of George Washington* (HarperCollins, 1993); Catherine Millard, *Great American Statesmen and Heroes* (Horizon Books, 1995); and Richard Brookhiser, *Founding Father: Rediscovering George Washington* (Free Press, 1996).

Daniel Boone

The Pathfinder

(1734–1820)

When Daniel Boone goes by, at night,
The phantom deer arise
And all lost, wild America
Is burning in their eyes.

—Rosemary and Stephen Vincent Benét
A Book of Americans

June 7, 1769

They had been riding up and down steep mountain ranges and through tangled forests and swamps for more than five weeks now, and still there had been no sign. As he changed his position in the saddle for the hundredth time, vainly seeking relief for his aching muscles, he wondered if they would ever find it. Perhaps the paradise the Iroquois called "Kanta-ke," or "land of meadows," was just a dream. At nearly thirty-five, he was too old to be chasing dreams. He ought to be back home in North Carolina helping around the farm and making sure that Rebecca, who was expecting their sixth child, wasn't trying to do everything for herself, as she tended to do. The vision of his wife's jet-black hair and dark eyes set against her fair skin was almost enough to make him turn around then and there.

But he stubbornly kept riding in the same direction. He and his five companions had come a far piece, and they had to see it through to the end, no matter what. They had set out on May 1, 1769. One of the party, an old friend named John Findley, had actually been to Kentucky, and he claimed that there was a "secret door" in the Appalachian Range that led the way. So, with about a dozen packhorses loaded with supplies and gear for hunting and trapping, they had traveled across the Blue Ridge Mountains to connect with the "Warrior's Path"—the route all the tribes used to travel between the east and the west on their raiding expeditions. When they reached the stretch of the Appalachians called the Cumberland Mountains, they looked for the "White Rocks"—the cliffs Findley said marked the little-known pass that would later become famous as the Cumberland Gap.[1]

---

1   Others had discovered it, but it was Daniel who would lead the first large groups of settlers through the Cumberland Gap; in succeeding decades, 300,000 settlers would follow in their wake.

After they successfully made it through the gap, they turned northward. But since no one in the group except Daniel was much of a woodsman, they had no real idea when they would get to their destination.

On this particular morning, they rode along a steep ridge between two rivers that gradually descended into some rather pleasant rolling hill country. Daniel took a deep breath and suddenly felt much more cheerful. The air was warm and smelled of wildflowers.

"Look there, fellers!" Findley cried excitedly. "I told you it was there all right. It's ol' Cantuck!" They pulled their horses up and dismounted. The high, conical-shaped hill on which they stood gave them a sweeping view of the landscape. It was Kentucky, no doubt about it. Never had such a place looked more like the Promised Land to Daniel. There were luxuriant meadows of tall green grass that went on seemingly forever. There were also thick hardwood forests and shining rivers and streams.

Daniel squinted hard and said, "Do you see that dark patch on the horizon?"

"It's black as night, and it must be at least a mile long. What can it be, Dan'l?" said John Stewart, a young man in his twenties who was married to one of Daniel's sisters.

"I have only seen the creatures once before, but never so many. There must be more than a thousand head in that single herd. 'What you're looking at, Brother John, are some of God's most mysterious and grand creations. They're called buffalo. Now, if you boys don't mind, I have a hankering to see them up close.' With sure and easy grace, he leapt into the saddle and galloped away toward the dream he had been chasing for so long."

H E WAS NOT OVERLY TALL, but he was powerfully built. According to one description, "He had his father's penetrating blue-gray eyes and fair, ruddy complexion but his mother's dark hair, which he always kept plaited and clubbed in Indian fashion." He wore a long, fringed leather hunting shirt and leggings made of the same material. He also sported a beaver hat with a narrow brim. Some of the other backwoodsmen he knew wore coonskin caps, but he thought they looked plain silly. Those who knew him well reported that his voice was "soft and melodious" and that he smiled a lot and was as gentle and mild-tempered as a lamb. But he was also said to be as brave and as tough as a mountain lion. Though he was a man of few words, people instinctively trusted and respected him. He was known for repeating mottoes, like "Better mend a fault than find a fault" and "If we can't say good, we should say no harm." An unusual character, indeed, was Daniel Boone.

He was born in a one-room cabin in a small village called Exeter near what is now Reading, Pennsylvania, on October 22, 1734. His father, Squire, was an English weaver who emigrated to America at age eighteen in 1713. His mother, Sarah, bore eleven children; she always claimed Daniel was her favorite. The Boones were members of the Society of Friends, or Quakers. This much-persecuted Christian sect was established in England in the mid-seventeenth century. Quakers did not hold with priests and believed that individual souls communicated directly with God. They advocated simple, almost spartan, living and a strict code of social and moral conduct. They also refused to let their members marry non-Quakers, whom they referred to as "worldlings." Although his wife Sarah remained a member, Squire Boone was expelled from the Society of Friends in 1748 after two of his children, Sarah and Israel, married outside the faith. Daniel decided to follow his father's example and leave the Society, but he remained a Christian. On all his explorations he carried a Bible, along with one of his favorite books, usually *Gulliver's Travels*.

He knew both practically by heart. On the subject of his faith, he once wrote in a letter, "How we live in this world and what chance we shall have in the next we know not. For my part, I am as ignorant as a child. All the religion I have is to love and fear God, believe in Jesus Christ, do all the good to my neighbor and myself that I can, and do as little harm as I can help, and trust on God's mercy for the rest and I believe God never made a man of my principle to be lost."

He grew up in the midst of a large extended family. His grandparents, aunts, uncles, and cousins all lived nearby. They were a fiercely loyal and affectionate clan. They taught Daniel the importance of taking care of one's "kith and kin." He may or may not have had a little formal schooling, but what is certain is that he learned to read and write when he was thirteen. Life was mainly filled with hard manual labor for the young boy. Every day, he had a long list of chores to perform. Around the cabin, he minded his younger brothers and sisters, churned butter, boiled lye and lard for soap, tanned hides, cured meat, cut firewood, and hauled water. In his father's blacksmith shop, he tended the bellows, mended harnesses, repaired traps and guns, and fashioned iron tools. In the fields, he herded stock, drove an ox-driven plow, planted seeds, and harvested crops. No moment was wasted; even when he was finally allowed to go into the forests he loved, it was to gather nuts from the hickory, walnut, and butternut trees or to hunt game for the supper table. Daniel learned to shoot like a expert marksman by the time he was fifteen. Indeed, in an era when most backwoodsmen were highly proficient with the "long rifle," a Pennsylvania innovation accurate up to distances of two hundred yards, his skill was widely considered extraordinary.

In many respects, however, Daniel was still just a normal youngster who liked to indulge in a bit of mischief now and then. When he was only four years old, he and his six-year-old sister Elizabeth were confined to the cabin during a deadly smallpox epidemic. They slipped out to visit a sick friend, intending, as he recalled many years later, "to take the smallpox, and when over it, be free to go where they pleased." Though it might have meant their death, their plan worked out just as they thought it would. On another occasion, Daniel left home for two days without a word to anyone. He had a wonderful time roaming the wilderness while his relatives frantically searched for him. They thought he had been killed by Indians or wild animals. Just as they were about to call off the search, they found him, hale and hearty, feasting on a bear he had shot. This was a theme that would be repeated again and again in Daniel's life: Many times he was given up for dead, but he always turned up.

In 1750, Squire Boone and other members of the Boone clan loaded up their Conestoga wagons and left Pennsylvania for the "western lands" in Virginia. They had no clear idea where they would settle; they simply knew that opportunity beckoned. Pulling up stakes and moving to an unknown territory after hearing wondrous tales about it—this would be another persistent theme in Daniel's life. One biographer pointed out that he must surely have felt as if his family was living out the biblical story in which the Hebrews journeyed to the land of Canaan. The green and fertile Yadkin Valley of North Carolina, which they reached in 1751, seemed like an answer to their prayers. Daniel helped his parents with the arduous task of clearing land, building a cabin, and planting crops.

IN THE FALL, he and his best friend, Henry Miller, went on their first "long hunt," which took them all the way to the Shenandoah and Blue Ridge Mountains. They had no detailed maps to guide them; they simply followed the trails they found, and sometimes they even blazed their own. Each boy carried only the essentials: rifle, powder horn, lead, bullet mold, hunting knife, hatchet, and tinder box. A packhorse carried a cast-iron kettle, traps, salt, and a few provisions like cornmeal. For months, Daniel and Henry hunted bear, raccoon, turkey, pigeon, otter, muskrat, and elk, but they concentrated mainly on deer and beaver. When they had a big enough cache, they took the hides and furs they had dressed to faraway Philadelphia to sell. The "long hunt" was an Indian tradition many American pioneers adopted. After his first experience, Daniel knew he had found his vocation. He went on a long hunt nearly every fall for the next four decades. He called it his "business of life."

But he was also said to be as brave and as tough as a mountain lion. Though he was a man of few words, people instinctively trusted and respected him.

When he was much older, he learned to speak a "pidgin tongue based on Algonquian employing many English, French, Dutch, and Scandanavian terms that served as the lingua franca of the forest," but now he concentrated on learning to read the pictographs blazed on tree trunks along the trails. These "constituted a simple but common written language." He also learned to identify a wide variety of trees, plants, and herbs as well as the habits of many animals, and he came to know intimately the patterns of the seasons and the geography of lands few men had ever seen. One might say that Daniel was one of America's earliest and foremost naturalists, so well versed was he in the science of studying the natural world. Sometimes he hunted alone and sometimes he teamed up with companions, white and Indian alike. He loved the solitude, but he also loved company. He was normally quiet, but could make quite a speech if called upon, and he told some pretty fine tall tales, too, while sitting around the campfire.

IN 1755, HOWEVER, the biggest event in his life would not be hunting or storytelling but combat. At twenty years of age, Daniel volunteered to serve as a blacksmith and wagonmaster under British General Edward Braddock during the French and Indian War. Daniel was on the same ill-fated expedition against the French stronghold, Fort Duquesne (near present-day Pittsburgh), as a young Virginia officer named George Washington. They were part of a mile-long column of more than a thousand soldiers headed toward the fort in July. Daniel drove a wagon that probably carried food, munitions, or cannon. Indian scouts from the Delaware tribe offered to lead the way, but they wanted to know who would own the territory once the French were driven out. Braddock insulted them by proclaiming that "no savage should inherit the land." So, the offer was withdrawn and the army moved blindly, without advance intelligence.

Some days it made only three miles since the soldiers were forced to clear and build the road as they went. Fife and drum, along with the noise of the roadbuilders and the bright red uniforms of the British regulars, meant there could be no element of surprise. When they were about ten miles from their objective, the French, and the Indians under their command, launched an ambush. Daniel, like George Washington, was disgusted when Braddock refused to fight frontier-style. From his position about a half mile in the rear, he witnessed the terrible slaughter of his countrymen. Some of the teamsters ran, but he held his horses for three hours before joining the general retreat. Days later, the ragged remnants of the army staggered into Fort Cumberland. But Daniel was not present; he had decided enough was enough and it was time to go home. First, he wanted to make a brief stop at his birthplace in Pennsylvania to visit with friends and relatives he had not seen in years. Crossing a bridge over the Juniata River, he was confronted by a huge Indian brandishing a knife. Daniel had no weapon. The Indian, who was drunk and belligerent, boasted he had taken many English scalps; now, he wanted to take Daniel's. The two men struggled. Daniel was terrified and sure he would be killed. But he caught his opponent off balance and threw him over the side of the bridge. The Indian fell to his death.

This was an even more shattering experience than the bloody battle he had just witnessed. Daniel shared the Quaker reverence for life. Though he had acted in self-defense, he felt he had committed a great sin. He resumed his journey, but he told no one what had happened. The only time he would discuss the incident was once as an old man, and he recalled it with great regret. He was no Indian hater, despite the legends that have portrayed him as such. He had grown up among Quakers who negotiated with Indians over lands, treated them fairly, and did not organize militias against them. Daniel's grandfather had once rescued two Indian girls from white settlers. And it was a long-standing tradition for the Boones to welcome all travelers and offer them food and shelter, regardless of race. As a result, from an early age Daniel had a number of Indian friends and acquaintances.

He returned home to the Yadkin Valley after his nearly fatal encounter to find that his family was becoming quite prosperous. Squire Boone had been appointed justice of the peace and ran a tavern as well as a farm and blacksmith shop. He had also started a nondenominational church, or "meeting house," where he often led the services.

In August of 1756, Daniel married Rebecca Bryan, the daughter of a Welsh Quaker family that lived nearby. She was known for her piety, simplicity, and steadiness, as well as her beauty. Like many pioneer women, she was an experienced farmer, hunter, and housekeeper. Daniel and Rebecca used to tell their children that they began their courtship at a cherry picking. Daniel cut a hole in her best apron. Rebecca wasn't mad; she knew he was just trying to gain her attention. They had a real frontier wedding "shindig," attended by all the neighbors for miles around. Daniel was twenty-one, and Rebecca was seventeen. They built a log cabin near Farmington, North Carolina. There, in 1757, their son James was born. For the next several years, Daniel was a dutiful farmer and raised crops and cattle. But he did take time out to join the military expedition that finally took Fort Duquesne from the French. Then another son, Israel, was born. Altogether, Rebecca would bear ten children: James, Israel, Susannah, Jemima, Levina, Rebecca, Daniel Morgan, Jesse,

William (who died in infancy), and Nathan. She and Daniel would also raise more than half-a-dozen nieces and nephews who had lost one or both parents.

IN 1759, DANIEL RECEIVED WORD that the Cherokees were on the warpath and rushed his family to Fort Dobbs. He and Rebecca were filled with the "images of violent death that haunted the dreams of every border family." Fort Dobbs was dirty and overcrowded, and there was little food or water. The Boones were among the last to arrive and were told they must leave. So they fled north to Virginia. They lost their farm and all their possessions. To make ends meet, Daniel worked as a wagon driver on a tobacco plantation. Meanwhile, the attack on Fort Dobbs failed, but there was news of continuing Cherokee and Shawnee depredations throughout the region.

In 1762, Daniel and his family moved back to the Yadkin Valley, but things had changed. Settlers from the other colonies were pouring in; unclaimed land was getting more scarce and so was wild game. So, they kept moving westward until they were backed up against the Blue Ridge Mountains. Daniel explored Florida in the fall of 1765 with a party of long hunters. He would have moved there, but Rebecca refused to go. After giving up one homestead after another, she wanted to put down roots. By staying in one place, she reasoned, they might even be able to get ahead for once. But Daniel was restless and filled with wanderlust. The frontier beckoned to him like an irresistible force. While in the militia, he had befriended John Findley, an Irish teamster, who told him all about the largely unexplored land of Kentucky. It sounded like the Garden of Eden.

In the spring of 1769, Daniel set off with Findley and four others to explore Kentucky. They were not disappointed by what they found. Kentucky seemed to have everything they could desire, especially an abundance of buffalo, deer, beaver, and other wild game. For eight months, the party hunted and dressed hides and furs. They were well on their way to making a fortune. Then disaster struck.

December 22, 1769

Daniel woke up with a start, his palms sweaty and his heart pounding like a drum. He was not easily frightened, but the dream was so real that even now, fully awake, he could not shake off the feeling of foreboding that gripped him. He shrugged off his blankets and squatted before the dead coals of last evening's fire. Dare he light it again? What if there were Indians close by? He had not seen any sign for the past few months, but that counted for nought. Cherokees or Shawnees could show up anytime without warning; after all, this was their hunting ground. He decided to take a chance, and he took out his tinderbox. In a few minutes, he had a small, cheery blaze going. It helped lift his spirits a little. Warming his hands, he recalled his dream. His father, who had died four years earlier, was walking toward him. Daniel tried to embrace him, but his father pushed him away. The expression on his face was angry and full of warning. What could such a strange vision mean?

Soon, the other hunters were up, and it was time to start tanning the deer hides they had lately collected. This was a laborious and time-consuming process. The hides had to be thoroughly scraped with sharp knives. Every last speck of flesh or hair must be removed. It took Daniel's mind off his troubles. He soon forgot about his dream. At mid-day, he and his brother-in-law, John Stewart, took some time off to go into the woods and hunt for their supper. As they rode back to camp in the late afternoon, John said, "What's that noise?"

Daniel halted. "Probably some animal in the cane-brake over yonder, but we best make sure." He started toward the sound.

Suddenly, a group of mounted Shawnees broke cover and surrounded them, galloping wildly and waving their war clubs.

Daniel didn't panic. He raised his hand in a friendly gesture and said, "How do, brothers. I reckon you're out hunting on this fine afternoon. Any luck?"

"Much luck, indeed." The biggest and most fearsome-looking Indian in the group spoke English. "We have been hunting you. We have caught you, too. Now, show me your camp!"

Daniel and John led their captors to several of the sites where they had cached furs and hides, but the big Indian, whose English name was Captain Will, was not fooled. He insisted that they lead him to the main camp. After stalling as long as they could, they complied. Fortunately, the others hunters had heard all the ruckus and gone into hiding. The camp was deserted. The Shawnees took all the horses and the hundreds of furs and hides stored there as well. Then Captain Will gave each man two pairs of moccasins. He also gave Daniel a small quantity of lead and powder and a gun.

"These gifts I make to get you home safe. Now, brothers, go home and stay there. Don't come here anymore, for this is the Indians' hunting ground, and all the animals, skins, and furs are ours. And if you are so foolish as to venture here again, you may be sure the wasps and yellow jackets will sting you severely."

INSTEAD OF GOING HOME, Daniel and John tracked the Shawnees and tried to retrieve their goods. It was a bad idea; they were captured again the next day. Captain Will did not release them this time. He ordered them tied together and they were forced to march north. They were told they would be set free only after the party crossed over the Ohio River, but Daniel and John decided not to wait and escaped after about a week. The Shawnees did not pursue them. They returned to their base camp and laid low for several days. Then, happily, they chanced upon their missing campmates along with Daniel's brother (called "Squire" after their father) and another man, Alexander Neeley. Squire and Alexander had traveled four hundred miles and still managed to pick up their trail.

Part of the original group elected to return home, but Daniel, John, Squire, and Alexander decided to stay and trap for the rest of the winter. John disappeared without a trace one day. (Daniel would find his remains four years later on another expedition.) They were all greatly troubled, and Alexander was so frightened that he headed back to civilization. The two Boone brothers now had only each other for company. In the spring, Squire went home to trade furs for supplies. Daniel was completely alone in the wilderness for nearly three months. When Squire returned, it was with the news that Rebecca had borne a son, Daniel Morgan Boone, on December 23, the day after Daniel had first been captured by the Shawnees. They spent another year trapping. Again, Squire rode home with bales of deer hides and beaver pelts, and Daniel stayed behind. Roaming the forests, he explored the countryside and made maps, mainly in his head, of what he saw. He finally returned with Squire to North Carolina in 1771. He had been gone two years. But as he and Squire crossed the Cumberland Gap loaded with furs, Indians robbed them, and they returned home "with only the shirts on their backs—and lucky at that. It was the way of the wilderness."

In the spring of the same year, shortly before the Boones' return, a missionary stopped to see Rebecca. He recorded in his diary, "She is by nature a quiet soul, and of few words. She told me of her trouble, and the frequent distress and fear in her heart."

Imagine Rebecca's gladness when she stopped to rest for a moment from her chores and saw on the horizon a familiar-looking horseman approaching. When her husband came home, it must have been as if a heavy burden had been lifted from her shoulders. But the relief was only temporary; they had no money, so Daniel soon went on another long hunt, this time in Tennessee.

IN 1773, HE FINALLY CONVINCED the reluctant Rebecca to make the journey to Kentucky. Along with thirty to forty men, women, and children, they made camp on the eastern side of the Cumberland Gap. Then they sent their teenage son James, along with a few other young men to procure additional supplies and inform another group of settlers of plans for a rendezvous. On the return trip, they encountered a party of Delawares, Shawnees, and Cherokees who were on their way home from a secret intertribal council that had been called by the chiefs of each tribe to discuss how to discourage whites from encroaching onto Indian lands. Here, thought the Indians, was a perfect opportunity to send a signal that western settlement would not be tolerated. They set upon their victims without mercy. News of the attack quickly reached Daniel, but he could not leave the women and children without protection. So, Squire and several other men went to investigate. They found the bodies along the trail. The young men had been terribly tortured; the nails on their hands and feet had been torn out, and they had been beaten and shot with arrows. One of them was James. The massacre ended the first attempt to settle Kentucky. It also brought brutal retaliation and torture of Indians by a number of colonists, but not by Daniel. On the frontier, where violence begat violence and where vengeance was typically considered an honorable justification for murder, his remarkable restraint showed the true depth of his character.

Grief-stricken and homeless, Daniel, Rebecca, and the children holed up in an abandoned cabin in Virginia. Daniel and another woodsman traveled eight hundred miles in sixty days to find a party of surveyors in the Ohio Valley and warn them that a hostile Indian force was on the move. In 1774, he led the defense of the Clinch River settlements against the Shawnees during the campaign that was called "Dunmore's War" after the militant British governor of Virginia, the Earl of Dunmore. According to one story told by a woman at Moore's Fort, Daniel got his militia captaincy in a peculiar way. The men were very lax about defense and spent every day outside the gates. They "would all go out and play ball, and those that were not playing would go out and lie down, without their guns." Rebecca, her daughters Susannah and Jemima, and several other women decided to put a scare into them. They went outside the fort, fired a musket volley, and then ran back inside and barred the gates. There was no laxness after that, and Daniel was put in charge.

Daniel was one of America's earliest and foremost naturalists, so well versed was he in the science of studying the natural world.

But then real Indian attacks began. Daniel and a troop of fourteen rangers moved up and down the valley to all the forts, and "soon he became a familiar and comforting presence to the settlers the whole length of the Clinch." He had earned a reputation among a tough, independent breed of men and women who were awfully hard to impress "as the best man to call in an emergency." He took time away from his duties only once during this period to make a pilgrimage to the site where James had been killed. He dug up the bodies of all the slain young men, who had been hastily covered over, and buried them properly. "As he completed his work," says one account, "the late afternoon sky filled with dark clouds and a violent storm erupted. Boone sat by the side of the graves in the rain and wept. It was an experience he often recalled with his family, and during the telling it would be as if he was returned to the graveside once again."

When the war came to an end, the defeated Shawnee tribe ceded to Virginia its claims to Kentucky in a controversial treaty that, in a short while, both sides would violate. Daniel resigned from the militia; in 1775, he agreed to be an advance agent for Richard Henderson, who wanted to take advantage of the peace to found a settlement in Kentucky. Henderson was a North Carolina judge, colonel, and land speculator. He formed the Transylvania Company to make a deal with the Cherokees, who, like the Shawnees, also held claims on Kentucky. Boone arranged for a pow-wow. Despite angry protests from the most militant warriors, the Cherokee chiefs sold the rights to their historic hunting grounds. One of them said to Daniel, "Brother, it is a good land we have sold you, but you will find it hard to hold."

With a party of about thirty men, including some of Henderson's slaves, and two women, Daniel blazed the Wilderness Road that ran from Virginia to Kentucky.[2] It would endure as the main route to the west until 1840. Despite the peace, Shawnee attacks killed several men and wounded others. The rest of the party would have fled, but Daniel convinced them to keep going. Once they made it to the Kentucky River they relaxed, however, and he could not get them to build a fort. Anxious for profit, they just wanted to build a few cabins, hunt, and stake out claims. He clashed repeatedly over this issue with Richard Callaway, an arrogant, hot-tempered former militia colonel from Virginia.

When Richard Henderson arrived with reinforcements and supplies in the spring of 1776, Boonesborough, a rough, partially finished fort near present-day Lexington, was finally erected. Daniel went back to North Carolina for more settlers, including his own family. The proprietary government of the Transylvania Company, the only recognized authority in Boonesborough, was eventually disbanded when Kentucky was made a county of

---

2   One of the women was a slave owned by Richard Callaway and the other was Daniel's fifteen-year-old daughter Susannah. She had just married one of the party, Will Hayes. This perilous journey was actually her honeymoon trip.

Virginia. Boone was again elected captain of the militia, but he and the other members of the company lost their land claims and had to start fresh. They had more competition now, too; there were at least several hundred settlers in the region by this time. "Kentucky fever" outweighed fear of the Indians. A new era had begun, but it would not be an era of peace or prosperity.

July 14, 1776

"Come on, they'll hardly miss us, you 'fraidy cats. We won't be gone long. The water will be so cool and refreshing. I can hardly stand being cooped up in this dirty old pigsty of a fort any longer," thirteen-year-old Jemima Boone complained to her friends, Fanny and Betsy Callaway. Fanny was fourteen and Betsy was sixteen, but Jemima, with her vivacious and often mischievous ways, was the undeniable ringleader of the little group.

"Our paw would skin us alive, if he knew," Betsy protested.

"Listen to Jemima," Fanny pleaded with her older sister, "The river is close by, and all the grown ups are resting or reading indoors since it's the Sabbath. No one will know we have gone if we hurry."

Thus persuaded, Betsy overcame her misgivings, and the three girls slipped out of the fort. The broad blue Kentucky River was a beautiful sight after months of enforced confinement inside Boonesborough. The settlers had forted up after the body of a boy from the settlement had been found face down and scalped in a nearby cornfield. The carefree young girls did not spare a thought for this tragedy while they filled their aprons with sweet wild grapes and made wreathes of flowers for their hair.

"Look, there's an abandoned canoe," Betsy exclaimed. "Let's take it across to the other side."

"We mustn't," declared Jemima with an unexpected display of caution. Her father had warned her that she must never cross the river under any circumstances.

"Whose being the 'fraidy cat now? Why, you're afraid of those yellow boys!" Betsy teased. Now that she was free of the fort, she felt brave and rather reckless. She and Fanny jumped in the canoe. "Just push us off, and then you can run along home to your folks if you're too scared to go with us."

Jemima said disgustedly, "I suppose I'll have to go just to keep you out of trouble. Here, move over, Fanny, and I'll help your sister paddle."

The river swept them downstream quickly. Betsy steered hard toward a sycamore grove along the north shore where she hoped the current would be gentler. As they approached the bank, a huge figure leapt from behind the trees and charged into the water after them.

"Law! Simon, how you frightened me!" Fanny cried, thinking that she recognized him as a friendly Indian who lived at Boonesborough. But then she realized that it wasn't Simon. It was a strange brave with a terrifying expression and a raised tomahawk. All three girls screamed wildly for help as four more Indians materialized out of nowhere and grabbed the canoe. One of them seized Fanny by the hair and drew his knife. He made angry signs that he would scalp her unless they all quieted down. Shuddering with fear, the girls wept and moaned as the Indians bound their hands with leather thongs and led them roughly into the woods.

One of the Callaway boys who had also slipped out to take a stroll near the river heard the girls' cries. He raced back to the fort. "The savages have come!" Daniel, who had been resting on his bed half-dressed so as not to ruin his Sabbath clothes, grabbed his trousers and his rifle and ran barefoot to the river. A group of men, women, and children had gathered and everyone was talking at once. "Calm down!" he shouted above the din. "Now, who's missing?"

"Your gal, Jemima, plus my sisters," supplied the boy who raised the alarm. Within minutes, one group of men headed downriver on horseback toward a shallow ford. Another, led by Daniel, crossed in the canoe that had by this time been retrieved. They picked up the trail with little trouble; Jemima pretended to stumble every chance she got and broke branches that served as markers.

After some hours of hard going, the girls were allowed to stop for the night. They collapsed in a heap, too tired to struggle as they were tied to tree trunks. No food or water was offered. The leader of the group was an English-speaking Cherokee called Hanging Maw who had met Daniel and his family back in North Carolina. He recognized Jemima and asked, "Who are these girls with you?"

"My sisters," Jemima replied, thinking that he would refuse to harm an old acquaintance's daughters.

"Ha! We have done pretty well for old Boone this time," Hanging Maw laughed mirthlessly. "We are taking you far away to sell to our Shawnee brothers up north. You three will fetch a handsome price. Then, we will come back for the rest of your people. Boonesborough will be no more. The whites will leave Kanta-ke forever."

Jemima's heart sank. She knew that all hope of rescue would be lost once they were taken up north into the Ohio country. Worse yet, there would be no one to warn the fort of an impending attack.

Before first light, the Boonesborough search parties converged and were on the move again. But the trail was becoming more difficult to follow. Daniel finally spoke up.

"This will never do. The Indians are making tracks faster than we are. But I think I know where they are heading: the ford at the Upper Blue Licks on the Licking River. We can take a shortcut and catch up to them."

"How can you have the least idea where they are taking our girls?" Richard Callaway blustered. "I'm ten years your senior and, moreover, I was a colonel in the militia, so I outrank you. I order you to stick with the trail."

Flanders Callaway, who was also Jemima's suitor, sided with Daniel. "I think we ought to trust Cap'n Boone, Uncle Richard. He knows a heap more about this country than any man alive."

"Or so he claims," Callaway sneered. "Let's put it to a vote, then."

Not surprisingly, the men voted in favor of Daniel's plan. They traveled mile after mile, following his swift silent lead. Finally, they crossed the Indians' trail. But Daniel insisted that they keep going on a straight course. On the third day, they picked up the trail again, this time about thirteen miles from the Licking River.

"We're closing in," Daniel observed as he inspected the muddied water at a stream crossing. "The party we're looking for is no more than an hour ahead of us." He sat down on the bank, yawned, and then stretched out full length on the grass.

"What are you doing?" Richard Callaway said incredulously. "You just said we've nearly got them, and here you are preparing to take a nap. You must be mad!"

"All things in season," Daniel said imperturbably as he crossed his arms above his head and closed his eyes. He appeared to drift off into a peaceful sleep almost immediately while Callaway stood by fuming. The other men were also upset by Daniel's behavior, but they followed his example and bedded down for a rest.

The smell of roasting buffalo on the spit was enticing, especially since they had gone without food for days. The girls huddled together in front of the fire. One of the braves came up to Betsy and playfully tugged her hair. That shook Betsy out of her stupor and, without hesitation, she picked up a piece of bark, scooped up a load of hot coals, and dumped it on his moccasins. While the brave danced around in agony, Hanging Maw laughed and said, "Fine young squaw!"

Meanwhile, Jemima was peering into the trees. She couldn't believe her eyes. There was her father, creeping upon his breast like a snake toward the camp. He had come! Now everything would be all right.

Suddenly, a shot rang out.

Daniel was furious; someone in the rescue party had gotten nervous and fired before the signal was given. He jumped to his feet and began running. He saw Jemima push the Callaway girls to the ground. "Good girl. You remember what I taught you," he said to himself as he took aim with his rifle. Missed. That was all right; the Indians were fleeing, and all he wanted was to ensure the safety of the captives. Then, with horror, he saw Betsy stand up and start running. In the dark with her long black hair, she would be mistaken for an Indian. And there, sure enough, was one of the men about to club her with the butt of his gun. Daniel roared, "Stop! Don't kill her when we have traveled so far to save her!" He rushed in and knocked the rifle aside. The man who had nearly killed Betsy fell to the ground, sobbing. Daniel patted his shoulder and said in a bracing tone, "There now, no harm was done. Thank Almighty Providence, boys, for we have the girls safe. Let's all sit down by them now and have a hearty cry."

Years later when she told the tale to her grandchildren, Jemima would recall, "There was not a dry eye in the company."

THERE WAS GREAT REJOICING when the rescued and the rescuers returned to Boonesborough. Three weeks later, Daniel, as justice of the peace, performed the first marriage ceremony in Kentucky, uniting Betsy Callaway and Samuel Henderson. Not long afterward, Jemima would marry Flanders Callaway. News reached the settlement in August of the same year that the colonies had issued the Declaration of Independence. There was a grand celebration that lasted several days. The Kentuckians prided themselves on their independence, but many were divided over the issue of whether to remain loyal to their mother country or side with the rebels. Rebecca's family, the Bryans, were well-known Loyalists, but Daniel decided to join the American cause. He was promoted to colonel in the militia. Still, he kept the proof of his captain's commission in the British colonial army. He made no secret of the fact that he was proud of his record of military service.

In 1777, he was wounded in a Shawnee attack on Boonesborough. He and a party of men including the soon-to-be-famous scout and Indian fighter, Simon Kenton, were just outside the fort when they were ambushed by Shawnees. Daniel took a bullet in the ankle and fell to the ground. One of his biographers tells what happened next, making painfully clear the terrible savagery of war:

> Tomahawk raised, an Indian jumped astraddle his [Daniel's] body, but from close quarters Kenton fired and the man collapsed by Boone's side. Another Shawnee ran up, his knife drawn, but Kenton lunged forward, swinging the breech of his gun, and crushed the man's skull. Hoisting Boone to his shoulders, Kenton ran toward the fort as bullets sang by his head and smashed into the stockade wall.

One of the Boonesborough settlers was killed and four others, including Daniel, were gravely wounded. Periodic attacks on the fort continued for another year—the third year in a row. The

settlers were demoralized and had been able to do very little farming or hunting. Their clothes were in rags, and the women and
children scavenged for edible green plants and nuts in the woods
while the men stood duty as sentries.

In January of 1778, Daniel and a party of men
made a trip, borne out of sheer desperation, to the
Blue Licks. They had to make salt, which was essen-
tial for curing meat. Without meat, Boonesborough
could not survive. Making salt meant boiling thousands of gallons of water at salt springs to come up
with a small supply. Returning from a hunt in
February, Daniel was captured by four Shawnee
braves. He had tried to run in the deep snow, but
was quickly overtaken. He was led to Chief
Blackfish's camp, which boasted over one hundred
warriors en route to Boonesborough. The settlers
would be caught off guard because Indians rarely, if
ever, campaigned in winter. It would be a massacre. But the ever-
resourceful Daniel had a plan. He led his captors to believe that he
was quite happy to join them. When Chief Blackfish revealed that
he planned to kill the rest of the salt makers back at the Blue Licks,
Daniel promised that he would convince them to surrender peacefully. He also pledged that Boonesborough would surrender in
the spring. Chief Blackfish agreed. In return, Daniel extracted a
promise from the chief that none of the salt makers would be
forced to run the "gauntlet," a line of warriors armed with sticks
and clubs. But he forgot to include himself, so the wily Indian
made Daniel run instead.

All twenty-seven salt makers were marched to the northern
Indian town of Chillicothe on the Little Miami River and then to
Detroit, pending sale to the British, who maintained a garrison
there. Even with his fellow captives, Daniel kept up the pretense of
being content with the Indians. He showed British General
Hamilton his old commission as a militia captain in the British

**Daniel's grandfather
had once rescued
two Indian girls
from white settlers.
And it was a long-
standing tradition
for the Boones to
welcome all travelers
and offer them
food and shelter,
regardless of race.**

army and repeated his promise to convince Boonesborough to surrender in the spring. Hamilton liked Daniel and offered one hundred pounds as a ransom, but Blackfish refused to part with him.
The Indians returned to Chillicothe and the chief adopted Daniel as
a son, ironically enough, to replace a son killed in Jemima's rescue.
Daniel was given the Indian name *"Sheltowee,"* or *"Big Turtle."*

For four months, Daniel bided his time and waited for the
right moment to make a daring escape.[3] It was just before dawn in
June of 1777. The warriors had been up all night participating in a
war dance and preparing for the long-delayed surprise attack;
Blackfish had decided that force was superior to negotiation after
all. Daniel slipped away and alternately walked and ran one hundred and sixty miles to Boonesborough in just four days. His
daughter Jemima told him the sad news that Rebecca had given
him up for dead and moved back to North Carolina. Daniel
wanted to head after her immediately, but he knew he first had to
coordinate Booneborough's defense. Fortunately, after Daniel's
escape, the Shawnees delayed their attack. They knew the element
of surprise would be gone. This allowed the settlers a few weeks to
gather emergency provisions and reinforce the stockade, which had
fallen into a shocking state of disrepair. Then, a force of nearly 450
Indians and French Canadians surrounded the fort, which held
sixty men and older boys, twelve women, and twenty children, and
demanded that the inhabitants surrender to "his Britannic
majesty." The tiny remnant stubbornly refused. Its members
returned fire when it was offered, prayed ceaselessly, and kept vig-
ilant watch. Jemima was hit by a sniper's bullet, but it was largely
spent by the time it reached her, so she suffered no real harm.
Daniel was hit in the shoulder, but it also was a superficial wound.

---

[3]   Most of the salt makers who had been adopted by the Indians were relatively
well treated and managed to escape within a year or two, but those who
were sold to the British had no such luck. They were put to hard labor or
imprisoned. Half of this group eventually escaped; the rest either died or
were released after the war.

The aggressors camped a half mile from the fort on September 7. Hoping to stall for time to allow reinforcements from Virginia to arrive, Daniel initiated a series of negotiations that lasted until September 9. In the meeting on that day, a fight broke out between Richard Callaway and one of the Shawnee chiefs. Suddenly, everyone began fighting. The delegates from the fort barely made it back inside the stockade alive; Daniel's back was torn open by, of all things, the "calumet," or peace pipe, they had been smoking with Blackfish. His brother Squire was shot in the shoulder. The Indians charged the stockade in wave upon wave, but the improvements Daniel had ordered helped it withstand the assault. Steady firing took place the next day. The Indians built a fire next to one wall, but in a display of heroism that was destined to become commonplace during the siege, one of the settlers dashed out and doused it with water. Squire, who was known to be inventive, devised "squirt guns" for the same purpose from old rifle barrels and even constructed a wooden cannon that not only worked but shook the Indians' confidence. Another unexpected bonus was the rainy weather; it was responsible for collapsing the tunnels the Indians dug to undermine the stockade walls and for putting out burning torches and arrows. The siege ended on the evening of September 17. The residents of Boonesborough had been vastly outnumbered but had held out for eleven days with only two fatalities. The Shawnees, by contrast, had lost nearly forty men, and so they gave up and went home.

He had done more than any other man to open up the western territory, and his fame spread throughout the nation.

Daniel had saved Boonesborough. But there were those like Richard Callaway who held long-standing grudges against him and who accused him of treason. Since Rebecca's family was loyal to the king, this seemed to give credence to the charge that he was secretly working for the British and their Indian allies. When a court martial was convened in October, Daniel refused legal counsel, choosing to represent himself. To many, this seemed like a suicidal course; the penalty for treason was death. But he was stubborn. Finally, he agreed to let several acquaintances sit on the defendant's bench with him and offer some limited legal advice. His accusers seemed to have a strong case. Daniel *had* ordered the salt makers at the Blue Licks to surrender. He *had* promised the Shawnees and the British that he would convince the settlers at Boonesborough to do the same. He *had* shown General Hancock his old captain's commission in the British army. But, in a stunning display of shrewdness and frankness, Daniel destroyed each of the charges against him by demonstrating how his actions had helped save lives and deceive the enemy. It had been a dangerous deception, to be sure, but it had worked brilliantly. He even managed to use the testimony of several of the prosecution's key witnesses to prove his innocence. The jury of military officers agreed that, without Daniel's intervention, the salt makers and the families at Boonesborough would have been killed. He was not only acquitted of treason but promoted to the rank of major.

At last, he was free to return to North Carolina to retrieve his family. In 1779, he brought Rebecca and the children as well as a large group of new settlers to a site about six miles from Boonesborough that was named Boone's Station. (Along for the journey was an old friend named Abraham Lincoln and his son, Tom. Tom would eventually marry another member of the party, Nancy Hanks, and they would name their first-born son Abraham in honor of his paternal grandfather. The son would grow up to be the sixteenth president of the United States.) They arrived with a foot of snow already on the ground. It was known as the "Hard Winter." Game and livestock froze to death. Daniel divided up the meager store of corn he had brought among all the families in the settlement. Somehow, they hung on, and Boone's Station grew. It was here in 1781 that Daniel and Rebecca's tenth child, Nathan, was born.

Indian attacks still occurred from time to time, and the brutality escalated. On a hunt in 1780, Daniel and his brother Edward were set upon by Shawnees. Edward was killed. Daniel escaped into the forest. He ran all night to fetch help. The next day when he returned, he found that the Indians had beheaded his brother; because of the family resemblance, they thought they had killed the famous Boone and wanted proof to show their tribe.

Daniel was elected to the Virginia legislature in the revolutionary government and arrived in Richmond in May of 1781, just as the local populace was preparing to retreat in the face of a British invasion. Daniel was captured when one of the Redcoats overheard a man call him by his military rank, but he played dumb and was eventually paroled as a noncombatant.

WHEN DANIEL FINALLY RETURNED to Kentucky in the winter of 1782, he and his family moved about five miles away from Boonesborough onto a farm owned by his brother Israel. He resumed farming and hunting. Boonesborough was growing like a weed; there were more settlers and more battles with the Indians. After nearly a decade of fighting, war had become a way of life. Kentucky had already gained a sinister nickname, "Dark and Bloody Ground." But 1782 was the worst year yet; it was referred to as the "Year of Blood." The Indians planned a massive assault on Bryan's Station, a fort with forty cabins not far from Boonesborough. According to one account, a huge Indian army surrounded the palisades that sheltered fifty men plus a large group of women and children. They had no water. The women and girls knew that if the men showed their faces outside the fort, they would be killed. In the morning, therefore, they opened the gate and went to the spring. They slowly and calmly filled their buckets, pretending that Indians all around them did not exist. Not long after they were safely inside, the Indians attacked. But reinforcements slipped through the cornfields and into the fort later the same day. By nightfall, the attackers gave up.

More reinforcements, including Daniel, his son Israel, and his brother Samuel, arrived. Then came Colonel Logan and his militia force. Logan wanted to rush after the retreating Indians. Daniel studied the trail and declared that it was a clear invitation to ambush. He refused to join the chase but then did so reluctantly when his honor was challenged. All three Boones were in the small advance party that followed the trail for about thirty-five miles to the Licking River, where they caught up with their quarry. Daniel counseled waiting for Logan and the main force, but again he was overruled. He and his son fought side by side at the Battle of Blue Licks. He saw Israel killed by an Indian named Big Jim. After all the losses he had suffered, this one seemed unendurable. But Daniel did not even have the luxury of grieving; he had to lead the retreat immediately or all the survivors in the advance party would be killed. Days later, he returned to help bury the dead. Their bodies had been rendered nearly unrecognizable by wolves, buzzards, and the summer heat. In the same battle, one of Daniel's nephews had been killed and another was crippled for life. "My footsteps have often been marked by blood," Daniel would reminisce years afterward. Kentucky was a wonderful country, but he noted that it had been "purchased with a vast expense of blood and treasure."

FINALLY, THE PEACE that signaled the end of the American Revolution in 1783 also marked the end of the worst of the Indian wars in Kentucky. Daniel was at Boone's Station when he heard the good news. Thus freed from military duty, he began to spend much of his time helping new settlers stake out their claims. He was careless about recording his own, and soon he was left without any property at all. But he had done more than any other man to open up the western territory, and his fame spread throughout the nation. A Lexington schoolmaster and land speculator named John Filson interviewed Daniel and published his story, *The*

Adventures of Col. Daniel Boone, in 1784 on his fiftieth birthday. It was a heroic epic, long on excitement and short on accuracy, but it captured his spirit and the spirit of the frontier. The story sold well enough in the United States, but in Europe it was "a minor sensation." Britain's most famous poet, Lord Byron, was inspired to immortalize Daniel in his poem, *Don Juan.*[4]

By this time, Daniel and Rebecca had moved to a settlement along the Ohio River to run a store and a tavern.[5] They moved several more times during the next sixteen years. Daniel tried a variety of pursuits, from surveying to land speculating. He also served two more terms in the Virginia legislature. But what pleased him most was that Rebecca began to go on long hunts with him. They worked well together, and both were more than content with this new phase in their relationship. Then their son Daniel Morgan told them that he had been granted a large parcel of land about forty miles from St. Louis in the Spanish territory of Missouri. The elder Daniel, filled with eagerness and optimism, longed to move west again. The long-suffering Rebecca approved, so he, too, applied for a land grant from the Spanish government in 1799. He made a *pirogue* (a fifty-foot canoe) to carry Rebecca, Jemima, Susannah, and the girls' families. Daniel led the group of men that drove the livestock all the way. He was sixty-four years old when they all arrived in St. Louis in July of

> **"Many heroic actions and chivalrous adventures are related of me which exist only in the regions of fancy.**
> **With me the world has taken great liberties, and yet I have been but a common man."**

---

4   In the 1820s through the 1840s, American writer James Fenimore Cooper wrote a number of novels like *The Last of the Mohicans* and *The Deerslayer,* which were based on Daniel's life and which became huge best sellers.

5   For the first and only time, Daniel bought slaves, like many other Kentucky residents who needed cheap labor. It was an era in which slavery was morally acceptable. Daniel had been a slave himself—to the Shawnees. Unlike many slave owners, in his everyday conduct he treated blacks as equals. Indeed, his closest friend and hunting companion in his later years was Derry Coburn, a slave owned by another member of the Boone family.

1800. The Spanish commandant welcomed him with great ceremony. But this honor was overshadowed by Susannah's death
from illness a few days later.

In exchange for encouraging more settlers to join him,
Daniel was given title to a large tract in the Femme Osage Valley,
and he was made the district magistrate. Though not "learned,"
he was considered prudent and evenhanded in his judicial decisions. One tale says he gave a cow of his own to a widow whose
cow he had to seize for nonpayment of debts. His most difficult
case involved the death of Will Hayes (Susannah's widowed husband and father of ten Boone grandchildren). Will was killed by
one of his son-in-laws, James Davis. Daniel handed down an
indictment of murder. There were extenuating circumstances,
however, so he personally accompanied the defendant to St.
Charles, posted a $3,000 bond, and provided testimony at the
trial, which ended in acquittal.

Daniel also spent the first few years of the nineteenth century
exploring Missouri and trapping and hunting. He had several
brushes with hostile Osage Indians. Once, he and his companion,
Derry Coburn, were forced to hide in a cave for twenty days. As
they collected their traps, preparing to head home, one snapped
shut on Daniel's hand. His injury was so serious that he and
Rebecca moved to a cabin on their son Nathan's property soon
afterward. It was here that they would learn that their daughters
Levina and Rebecca had died, both before the age of forty. They
sought comfort in the company of their only surviving daughter,
Jemima, who lived nearby.

When the United States completed the Louisiana Purchase
by buying over 800,000 square miles of western territory from the
Emperor Napoleon for $12 million in 1803, Daniel once again
lost all his property. In 1806, he went before the U.S. Federal
Land Commission to seek recognition for his Spanish land grant.
His petition was rejected in 1809. Despite this disappointment
and his ailing health, which was now marred by tuberculosis as

well as rheumatism, he did not give in. He immediately began working on another petition, this time to Congress. And in 1810, at the age of seventy-six, he embarked on a six-month expedition that reputedly went all the way to the Valley of the Yellowstone in northwestern Wyoming.

ON MARCH 18, 1813, Rebecca died after a brief illness. She was seventy-four years old. Daniel tried to behave stoically. He had lost so many loved ones, but this was the greatest loss of his life. Some measure of his indomitable and independent spirit slipped away. He made a point of paying off all his old debts. And he bought a coffin, which he took great pleasure in inspecting on a regular basis. He gave up his cabin and began dividing his time living among his children, Jemima, Daniel Morgan, Nathan, and Jesse. Strangers—we would call them "celebrity hounds" today— often came to talk with and gawk at the great frontiersman, but he usually managed to evade them. When he could not, he was unfailingly polite. When they asked, "Why Kentucky, Colonel Boone?" he always replied that he was just "naturally romantic." He was also quick to give credit to others: "It is true that I have suffered many hardships and miraculously escaped many perils, but others of my companions have experienced the same." Also among his visitors were a number of Shawnees who had befriended him when he was in captivity. Daniel repaid their affectionate regard by becoming a frequent visitor to their villages, which had been relocated to Missouri. Indeed, he often observed that the Indians were his most constant friends. But the Osage, as indicated earlier, were not at all hospitable, and on more than one occasion they massacred settlers. Daniel was one of the first on the scene at a neighbor's cabin where the children had been killed and the mother and father lay dying. Daniel, who was now in his mid-eighties, extracted a bullet from the man and a short while later picked up his rifle and lit out to find the Indians responsible.

As a result of Daniel's petition regarding his lands in Missouri, a special act of Congress was passed in 1814 that granted him one thousand acres. In 1817, he fell sick during his last long hunt. In Nathan's house in St. Charles, Missouri, just after sunrise on September 26, 1820, Daniel died quietly and peacefully in bed, a month before his eighty-sixth birthday. He was buried next to his beloved Rebecca. But even then, she couldn't get him to stay still; their remains were relocated to Frankfort, Kentucky, in 1845.

A modern biographer assessed Daniel this way: "He was a hero, but a hero of a new, democratic type, a man who did not tower above the people but rather exemplified their longings and, yes, their limitations." Another said:

> The life of a pioneer family was a comic-tragic drama of struggle and violence. Each one had many stories. The lives of these movers on the Wilderness Road and forest settlers were a rough and violent saga full of lights and shadows, sweet and bitter as the wild persimmon, rough and tough as the shag-barked hickories, fierce and tender as the tall waving corn of the valleys.
>
> Boone's story was the story of the whole people. It had all their griefs and tragedies and restless longings and rich half-fulfilled dreams, all their ranging freedom and mortal bondages. It rang with the roaring laughter and boisterous fun; it was dark with the unfathomable silent anguishes by new-made graves; it was full of lost hopes and dreams of grandeur. Through it rushed the winds and the voices....."We make our own destiny and we like it. We make our own glories and shames and we've just begun. Our songs and our dreams are made of the new moon over corn shocks, of the wind in the maple groves, of the silver-weathered rails in the fence along a prairie road."

The writers added, as if speaking directly to Daniel, "When history called for men of action you were there. And so your name still echoes in the mountain passes and is a whisper and a heartbeat along the old trail." But what did Daniel have to say about himself? He was humble, as always: "Many heroic actions and chivalrous adventures are related of me which exist only in the regions of fancy. With me the world has taken great liberties, and yet I have been but a common man."

SUGGESTED READINGS

The Court-Martial of Daniel Boone (Bantam Books, 1973) is a thoroughly researched and highly entertaining fictional account by Pulitzer Prize-winning author Allan W. Eckert. It centers on Daniel's trial after the siege of Boonesborough. John Mack Faragher's *Daniel Boone: The Life and Legend of an American Pioneer* (Henry Holt and Company, 1992) is a richly detailed biography that distinguishes between folklore and documented facts about Daniel's life. Most of this chapter simply summarizes Faragher's excellent work, although other sources consulted were James Daugherty, *Daniel Boone* (Viking Press, 1939); John Mason Brown, *Daniel Boone: The Opening of the Wilderness* (Random House, 1952); and Reuben Gold Thwaites, *Daniel Boone* (Corner House Publishers, 1977).

Louisa May Alcott

Union Nurse and Author

(1832–1888)

Far away there in the sunshine
are my highest aspirations.
I may not reach them,
but I can look up
and see their beauty,
believe in them,
and try to follow where they lead.

—Louisa May Alcott

October 1845

"Louisa! Louisa! Where have you gotten to? The washing won't do itself, you know."

The young girl sighed and rose from where she had been sitting on an old cartwheel that lay on its side in the yard. It was her favorite retreat. She had been doing chores and lessons since sun up, and her mother's half-teasing, half-scolding tone reminded her that she still had several hours' work ahead of her before "playtime" was allowed in the late afternoon. Since she was ten years old, she had been keeping a journal. Many of the entries read: "I rose at five, and after breakfast washed the dishes and helped Mother work....I ironed....We all went to the barn and husked corn....After my lessons I sewed till dinner...."

Her family had little, and she sometimes felt that it was hard to keep sunshiny and cheerful when life looked gloomy and full of troubles. In an entry at age twelve, she wrote, "More people are coming to live with us....I don't see who is to clothe and feed us all, when we are so poor now." She felt ashamed that her clothes were hand-me-downs and that her parents had to accept charity to keep food on the table. She tried to help out by sewing doll clothes to sell to other children in the neighborhood and by making candles from sheep tallow since the Alcotts couldn't afford whale oil for lamps.

But Louisa also managed to find happiness in the simplest pleasures. The morning after her mother called her to do the washing, she slipped out of the house in Concord, Massachusetts, before the dew was even off the grass. The moss under her feet felt like velvet as she ran under the arches of yellow and red leaves. She sang a little nonsense song that she made up purely for joy as she went along. Her heart was light, and the world seemed inexpressibly beautiful. Finally, out of breath, she halted at the edge of a great meadow and watched the rays of sunshine begin to spread over it. It was like going through a dark veil or grave into heaven beyond. A very strange and solemn feeling came over her as she stood there, with no sound but the rustle of the trees and the sun so glorious. It seemed as if she had never felt God so strongly before. She prayed in her heart that she might keep that happy sense of nearness in her life.

After a little while, it was time to head home where the inevitable chores and lessons waited. But she felt a sense of anticipation instead of dread. For who knew what adventure might lie around the next corner? Louisa loved to read and make up adventure stories. Often, she imagined she was a nomad wandering from one exotic place to another. This was not so implausible. With her masses of unruly chestnut curls, olive complexion, and dark, deepset eyes, she looked a little like a gypsy in a Romany caravan. And her family certainly did a lot of wandering. The Alcotts had moved from town to town all through her childhood. This was because her father, a kind but restless and improvident soul, seemed to have as hard a time settling down as he did earning a living.

But Louisa didn't just read and make up adventure stories. She wrote them down, too. She kept an "Imagination Book" in which she jotted down ideas and impressions as they came to her. From her youngest years, she had a great gift for spinning tales of romance and intrigue. Moreover, she had a way of making every one of them a kind of moral lesson. When she was fourteen years old, she wrote a poem called "My Kingdom" that shows her blooming talent as well as her intense interest in the moral life:

A little kingdom I possess
Where thoughts and feelings dwell,

And very hard I find the task
Of governing it well.
For passion tempts and troubles me,
A wayward will misleads,
And selfishness its shadow casts
On all my words and deeds.

How can I learn to rule myself,
To be the child I should—
Honest and brave—nor ever tire
Of trying to be good?
How can I keep a sunny soul
To shine along life's way?
How can I tune my little heart
To sweetly sing all day?
Dear Father, help me with the love
That casteth out my fear!
Teach me to lean on thee, and feel
That thou art very near;
That no temptation is unseen,
No childish grief too small,
Since thou, with patience infinite,
Doth sooth and comfort all.

I do not ask for any crown
But that which all may win,
Nor seek to conquer any world
Except the one within.
Be thou my guide until I find,
Led by a tender hand,
The happy kingdom in myself,
And dare to take command.[1]

---

1   In the fictional episodes in this chapter, I have tried to use Louisa's own
words as much as possible. They are from her journal and correspondence
but are not always presented as quotations.

L OUISA MAY ALCOTT was born on November 29, 1832, in Germantown, Pennsylvania. Her father, Bronson Alcott, was a schoolmaster and philosopher who wrote pioneering essays on education, child-rearing, and the yet unrecognized field of child psychology. He numbered among his closest friends such famous writers as Nathaniel Hawthorne, Walt Whitman, Ralph Waldo Emerson, and Henry David Thoreau. He, Emerson, and Thoreau were members of an intellectual movement called "Transcendentalism." They believed that it was possible to bring out the good in human nature through self-reliance, self-discipline, and self-examination. They also believed the natural world was divine. And they fought for women's rights and the abolition of slavery. Louisa's mother, Abba, was related to John Hancock, the chief signer of the Declaration of Independence. Although she came from one of Boston's oldest and most aristocratic families, she lived in genteel poverty before and after her marriage. She was a talented amateur writer and intellectual in her own right. She also assisted her husband in founding several schools and was forever busy taking on volunteer projects in the community and managing a large household.

The Alcotts were firm believers in the benefits of education, and they opened the Temple School in Boston as a kind of model Transcendental institution in 1834. Louisa was too young to attend. As she grew, she spent her days roaming freely about the city, making friends among its most exalted and humble residents. She ate gingerbread in fashionable shops with patrician old gentlemen. She sat on back alley stoops and listened to the gossip of washerwomen and scullery maids. She was once saved from drowning in a pond by a passing boy. On another occasion, when she tried to find her way home after a day of wandering, she became lost; the family had recently moved to a new neighborhood. Her parents became so alarmed that they persuaded the town-crier to travel along his route shouting that he was looking for "a little girl, six years old, in a pink frock, white hat, and new green shoes." Late in the evening, he was rewarded by the joyous cry, "Why dat's me!" from Louisa, who was sitting half-asleep on the doorstep of a vacant house with her arm around a stray dog she had acquired somewhere along the way.

The Temple School was closed in 1839 after Bronson was publicly criticized for exhibiting lenient discipline (he seldom if ever used the birch-rod to punish erring students as was the harsh practice of the day), discussing childbirth in the classroom, and admitting a black student. He moved his family to a small tenant farm in Concord, Massachusetts, in 1840. A strong advocate of combining intellectual and manual labor, he planned to give lectures and cut wood (for one dollar a day) to make a living. But the country was in the middle of a financial panic and there was little work to be had. To make matters even more difficult, he now had two additional mouths to feed: Louisa and her older sister, Anna, had been joined by Lizzie and May. Bronson was seized by despair. Impulsively, he decided to borrow funds from his long-suffering friend, Emerson, and travel to Europe to see if he could establish himself as a philosopher there. The seventeen months he was away were especially lonely and bitter for Abba, who felt that he had abandoned her and the children.

Louisa missed her father's stimulating conversation and generous affection, but she also loved the freedom of her new life in Concord. She explored the countryside whenever her chores and lessons permitted. She soon acquired a reputation for being a thoroughgoing tomboy.[2] "I always thought I must have been a deer or a horse in some former state because it was such a joy to run," she wrote in her journal. Abba regretted Louisa's apparent lack of interest in becoming a fashionable young lady and called

---

2   Even as an adult, Louisa "hated the paraphernelia of adult femininity. Gloves, bonnets, and done-up hair gave her terribly to worry. It was easier for her to shoulder a heroic responsibility than to accept a daily routine of hairpins."

her a "wild Indian" and a "hoyden," but she also admired her daughter's independent spirit since it was akin to her own. At this time, Louisa began to express her nature in a way that had nothing to do with climbing trees or racing through the fields. She began writing poetry and stories. Her father had taught her and Anna the alphabet by lying "on the floor with his long legs up in the air so they could 'write' with these 'pencils.'" Her mother had encouraged her literary aspirations with such treasured, and scarcely affordable, gifts as a pencil box and paper on which to record her thoughts. And she frequently placed inspirational little notes on Louisa's pillow where she would find them at bedtime. In return, Louisa shared her journal. One day, she found written under the last entry:

> MY DEAREST LOUY,—I often peep into your diary, hoping to see some record of more happy days. "Hope and keep busy," dear daughter, and in all perplexity or trouble come freely to your
> MOTHER.

Louisa wrote back:

> My DEAREST MOTHER,—You *shall* see more happy days, & I will come to you with my worries, for you are the best woman in the world.

When, as a teenager, Louisa complained bitterly that she lacked the privacy of a room of her own, her mother responded:

> Patience dear, will give us content, if nothing else...try to be happy with the good things that you have. They are many,— more perhaps than we deserve, after our frequent complaints and discontents.
>
> Be cheerful my Louy, and all will be gayer for your laugh, and all good and lovely things will be given to you....

AS ABBA RECOGNIZED, Louisa's journal was much more than a simple chronicle of events. It was the primary vehicle for examining her own character. When she first began keeping a journal at age ten, she wrote with a level of perception and concern that was beyond her years: "I was cross today, & I cried when I went to bed. I made good resolutions & felt better in my heart. If only I *kept* all I make, I should be the best girl in the world. But I don't, and so am very bad." Later, as an adult, she would add: "I used to imagine my mind a room in confusion, & I was to put it in order; so I swept out useless thoughts and dusted foolish fancies away, & furnished it with good resolutions & began again. But cobwebs get in. I am not a good housekeeper & never keep my room in nice order."

But Louisa's biggest worry—one that would haunt her for years—was what to do to save her family from impending disaster. The Alcotts were perpetually dependent on charity. The situation worsened when Bronson returned from England in 1842, bringing with him a new friend and a new philosophy called "utopianism." He and an Englishman named Charles Lane had decided to establish a communal farm called "New Eden" that would be based on a socialist economy. The experiment lasted only eight months before it became clear that socialism, even when established for the loftiest and most humane reasons, is destined to fail. In her journal, Louisa wrote of the barren, hard existence on the farm, subsisting on bread, squash, potatoes, apples, and water, and taking lessons from the cold and humorless Mr. Lane. She also poured out her fears about the welfare of her family. Bronson spoke openly of separation from his wife, even in front of his young daughters. He wanted to join a Shaker community in New York in order to pursue a life of pure contemplation. He may have even had a nervous breakdown as it became evident that New Eden was doomed. Abba was certainly on the verge of having one. She was exhausted from doing most of the daily work required to keep the commune going, and she felt unappreciated by her husband, Mr. Lane, and the other members.

Yet Bronson and Abba loved each other deeply, and the breach between them was eventually healed. In late 1844, the family moved back to Concord. Due to a small inheritance Abba received, there was enough money to travel by way of the recently opened railroad. It was an exciting trip, for the Alcotts had never ridden on a train before. Louisa loved feeling the speed (a "breakneck" pace of fifteen to twenty miles per hour), gazing at the swiftly passing scenery, and hearing the loud chug-chug of the steam engine. They soon bought their first home, "a picturesque brown cottage" christened "Hillside." (Years later, it would be the model for the March family's home in *Little Women*.) Louisa would live there from age thirteen to sixteen, during "the happiest years of her life" and "the happiest for the whole family." Her father began traveling to distant states on extended lecture tours that paid next to nothing but that provided a much-needed outlet for his energies. Abba and the girls lived off the garden, the orchard, and small loans from friends and relatives. Anna and Louisa attended Henry David Thoreau's Concord Academy for instruction in such subjects as geometry, algebra, grammar, and geography. In 1850, the entire household caught smallpox from some poor immigrants Abba had taken in. Fortunately, everyone survived. (Epidemics were dreaded with good reason. The year before, over one thousand Americans had died from a single outbreak of cholera.)

> **But Louisa's biggest worry—one that would haunt her for years—was what to do to save her family from impending disaster.**

When the family finances reached rock bottom, Abba finally decided to flout convention and move to Boston in order to earn a living.[3] She became a social worker in the poorest tenement neighborhoods. She collected and distributed food, clothing, and Bibles. But

---

[3] Most nineteenth-century women were not expected to have a career outside the home, and if they belonged to the "upper classes," as Abba did, they risked their respectability when they sought employment.

she quit after a few months when she disagreed with her employers, who wanted her to give aid to the shiftless as well as the needy. Regarding her next business venture, Louisa's journal recorded:

> 1852.—High Street, Boston.—After the small-pox summer, we went to a house in High Street. Mother opened an intelligence [employment] office, which grew out of her city missionary work and a desire to find places for good girls. It was not fit work for her, but it paid; and she always did what came to her in the way of duty or charity, and let pride, taste, and comfort suffer for love's sake.
>
> Anna and I taught, Lizzie was our little housekeeper,—our angel in a cellar kitchen, May went to school, father wrote and talked when he could get classes or conversations. Our poor little home had much love and happiness in it, and was a shelter for lost girls, abused wives, friendless children, and weak or wicked men. Father and Mother had no money to give but gave them time, sympathy, help; and if blessings would make them rich, they would be millionaires. This is practical Christianity.

She and Anna also volunteered to teach reading and writing three evenings a week to illiterate servants and ex-slaves. As one biographer said, "Their spare life brought home the lesson they had been taught from birth: However little they had, they must give a share of it to those who had less." Louisa also wrote about this period:

> ...I washed dishes & cooked in the basement kitchen, where my prospect was limited to a procession of muddy boots.
>
> Good drill, but very hard; & my only consolation was the evening reunion when all met with such varied reports of the day's adventures we could not fail to find amusement & instruction.
>
> Father brought news from the upper world, & the wise and good people that adorned it; mother, usually much dilapidated because she would give away her clothes, with sad tales of suffering & sin from the darker side of life....Then we youngsters adjourned to

the kitchen for our fun, which usually consisted of writing, dressing, & acting a series of remarkable plays….But we were now beginning to play our parts on a real stage, and to know something of the pathetic side of life, with its hard facts, irksome duties, many temptations, and the daily sacrifice of self. Fortunately, we had the truest & tenderest of guides & guards, & so learned the sweet uses of adversity, the value of honest work, the beautiful law of compensation which gives more than it takes, & the real significance of life.

Louisa organized plays to lighten everyone's attitudes. Over the years, she and her sisters wrote, acted, and sewed costumes for such melodramas as *Norna, or the Witches' Curse; The Captive of Castile, or the Moorish Maiden's Vow; The Greek Slave; Bianca;* and *The Unloved Wife, or Woman's Faith.* Colorful, larger-than-life heroines, heroes, villains, and buffoons populated the exciting worlds they created. Louisa was shy in the presence of strangers but bold in the roles she assumed. Anna recalled that they "usually acted the whole play, each assuming five or six characters, and with a rapid change of dress becoming in one scene a witch, a soldier, a beauteous lady, and a haughty noble….Of the world [we] knew nothing….Love was a blissful dream; constancy, truth, courage, and virtue quite everyday affairs of life."

Unfortunately, their parents seemed to be living proof that love is not always a blissful dream and that the everyday affairs of life are often full of strife. Abba's employment office failed. She simply could not find prospective employers to hire her clients, so she had to resort to taking in boarders. Bronson once again deserted the family and rented rooms across town in which he gave public lectures for a little remuneration. Louisa prayed nightly that the family would not be torn apart by poverty and discord. Adding to her unhappiness was the fact that she felt like a "caged seagull" in Boston. The "bustle, dirt, and change" of the city sent "all lovely images and restful feelings away." She found a job as a teacher to help make ends meet, but her heart wasn't in it. She confided: "School is hard work, & I feel as though I should like to run away from it. But my children get on; so I travel up every day and do my best. I get very little time to write or think; for my working days have begun."

When school was not in session, she worked as a menial servant. In one housemaid's position that lasted almost two months, she reported that she was "starved and frozen" and only earned the pitiful sum of four dollars from a callous, demanding employer. She was more pleased to work for another family for about six months as a "second girl." She wrote afterward, "I needed the change, could do the wash, and was glad to earn my $2 a week. Home in October with $34 for my wages. After two day's rest, began school again with ten children." In the evenings, she worked as a seamstress to earn extra income. It is easy to imagine a tall dark girl with an earnest face and melancholy eyes plying her needle and thread in the dim lamplight while she concocted stories in her head.[4] She gave almost all her salary to Abba to spend on the family. She kept just enough for the barest necessities. She ate sparingly, and she denied herself any luxuries, although the lavish displays in every Boston shop window tempted her greatly. She even refused to buy material to make new dresses, even though hers, which had been cast-offs when she acquired them, were now so old and worn that she was ashamed to be seen in them.[5] She also con-

---

[4] As a woman in her twenties, Louisa was described by various acquaintances as "taller than average," with dark chestnut hair that fell to her knees when it was unpinned. "She wore black or claret-colour as a rule, never blue. The style of her dress was plain and quaint." Upon meeting her, one young man was struck by her "earnest face, large dark eyes, and expression of profound interest in other things than those which usually occupy young ladies...." It was also reported: "In company she had a way of placing herself in a corner and looking out over the heads of the company at what was going on." Such vivid descriptions remind the reader of Louisa's literary self-portrait, Jo March, in *Little Women*.

[5] Louisa missed out on many events she longed to attend because she had nothing to wear. She found her lack of a suitable wardrobe especially mortifying because she already felt like an "oddity" and an "eccentric."

sciously decided to discourage any would-be suitors, telling herself sternly that romance was all fine and good when it flowed from the tip of her pen, but she was a working girl with an entire family to support. Love and marriage were another luxury she could ill afford.

Louisa consoled herself by poring over her favorite reading material, including John Bunyan's *Pilgrim's Progress,* Charles Dickens's *Oliver Twist,* Sir Walter Scott's *Kenilworth,* Carlyle's *French Revolution,* Goethe's poems, Plutarch's *Lives,* Milton's *Paradise Lost,* Johann von Schiller's plays, Charlotte Brontë's *Jane Eyre,* Harriet Beecher Stowe's *Uncle Tom's Cabin,* and Ralph Waldo Emerson's poems. And there were advantages to working in such a grand metropolis as Boston that were available to everyone—even those like Louisa who were living in reduced circumstances. She was able to hear such famous authors as William Thackeray and Charles Dickens lecture on their American tours. Attending the theater also became a "part of her education, a source for her writing, and a much-needed antidote to the hardships of her life." And she met the leading scholars and activists of New England and was welcomed into their circle. She thus found herself in the very center of debate about the issues that were most important to her: women's suffrage, social reform, and abolitionism. Moreover, each and every day she could see examples of young women just like her who were breaking barriers of convention to become nurses, doctors, teachers, writers, editors, and philanthropists.

She was so caught up in her first great work that she did not realize that chaos *was* coming: a bloody and violent civil war that profoundly changed her life as well as the lives of all other Americans.

Louisa hoped to join their ranks. In 1851, her first published poem, "Sunlight," appeared in the nation's most popular ladies' magazine, *Peterson's,* under the pen name of Flora Fairfield. And, in 1854, the *Saturday Evening Gazette* published a Flora Fairfield romance, "The Rival Prima Donnas." The twenty-one-year-old

Louisa called such work "rubbish," because it was not classic literature in the style of the great authors whom she admired. But it was valuable rubbish all the same; the *Gazette* paid her $10. In the same year, a collection of fairy stories she had written at age sixteen appeared as a slim volume titled *Flower Fables*. The messages of these poetic stories are summed up by a modern reviewer: Love is stronger than fear. Spiritual beauty is more important than physical beauty. Cruelty and selfishness demand atonement. Repentance and reformation bring content and peace.

After several years of moving back and forth between Boston and Walpole, New Hampshire, the Alcotts returned once again to Concord in 1857. They moved into Orchard House (another beloved home that would someday figure in *Little Women*) a year later. Louisa helped the family settle in, but then she prepared to go back to Boston on her "usual hunt for employment." She wrote with some trepidation that she seemed "to be the only breadwinner just now." The responsibility weighed heavily on her shoulders. She filled her battered trunk with her threadbare wardrobe, a pile of treasured books, and twenty-five dollars she had earned by writing magazine stories. When she arrived in Boston, she searched until she found a "sky parlor" for rent on the top floor of an old boardinghouse.[6] It was bare and drafty. The only view out the grimy windows was of hundreds of brown smoking chimneypots. It may have seemed dreary to most people, but to Louisa it was a wonderful sanctuary. It was hers and hers alone. She relished the feeling of independence it gave her. She worked diligently teaching, sewing, dusting, and sweeping for anyone who would hire her, and, of course, she wrote stories whenever she had a few free moments.

---

[6] Between 1856 and 1857, she tried a variety of living arrangements: renting rooms, boarding with relations, and working as a live-in governess. Only the first gave her the privacy she desperately desired, but at three dollars a week it was too expensive to continue for long.

But before the year was out, Louisa discovered she was urgently needed back in Concord. Lizzie, "the friendly child who loved the rainbow, shadows on the brook, the rustling breeze," had never fully recovered from a bout of scarlet fever that she had contracted from one of Abba's charity cases several years earlier. Now, she was wasting away despite anything the Alcotts or the doctors could do. In February of 1858, Louisa wrote about the beloved invalid in her journal: "Lizzie makes little things, and drops them out of the windows to the schoolchildren, smiling to see their surprise." But she also noted that her sister's interest in life was fast disappearing. She refused to eat and was often wracked by fever. Louisa and her mother began to nurse their patient round the clock. A month later, she died at age twenty-three.

> As a feverent abolitionist, Louisa longed to join the parade of men trooping off to war.

Soon after the funeral, Louisa, who was only twenty-five herself, mourned the loss of two more family members: Anna announced her engagement to a young man by the name of John Pratt and May took a job in Boston. She was left all alone with her parents, rattling around in a big empty house filled only with bittersweet memories. She was in a dazed state for weeks and wrote nothing that sold. The "Alcott Sinking Fund," as she referred to the family's small store of cash, was reduced to extinction. She contemplated going on the stage, which would have ruined her reputation. Then she contemplated worse. Standing on the edge of the mill-dam along the Concord River, she thought for one brief moment about drowning herself. But it would have been a cowardly act, she knew. Wearily, she turned her back on the dark roiling waters and trudged home. She wondered how she would ever get on with the dreary business life had become. Then, one Sunday morning, she went to hear her favorite preacher, Theodore Parker, deliver a sermon on "Laborious Young Women." It was about the need to adopt a vocation. Parker urged working women not only to earn a living but also to dedicate themselves to the ideals of

Christian service.[7] Louisa sat straight up in the pew. She was electrified by Parker's simple yet powerful message. It seemed heavensent to rescue her from despondency. "Under this one sermon," according to a biographer, she "built a whole new house of life." In November of 1858, she testified regarding her new outlook:

> The past year has brought us first death and betrothal,—two events that change my life. I can see that these experiences have taken a deep hold & changed or developed me. Lizzie helps me spiritually, & a little success makes me more self-reliant. Now that Mother is too tired to be wearied with my moods, I have to manage them alone & am learning that work of head and hand is my salvation when disappointment or weariness burden and darken my soul.
>
> In my sorrow, I think I instinctively came nearer to God & found comfort in the knowledge that he was sure to help when nothing else could.
>
> A great grief has taught me more than any minister, & when feeling most alone I find refuge in the Almighty Friend.

And there was good news soon to come on two other fronts. First, Bronson Alcott finally found steady employment as the superintendent of Concord schools. It was a job for which he was perfectly suited since it allowed him to travel from school to school (on foot since he couldn't afford a horse or a carriage), to give public lectures, to teach occasional classes, and to put his now more widely accepted educational theories into practice. Second, Louisa's stories were at last beginning to sell again. The *Saturday Evening Gazette, Gleason's Pictorial Drawing Room*

---

7   Theodore Parker was one of Louisa's mentors who would appear as the saintly Dr. Powers in her 1873 novel, Work. He believed that Christian principles ought to be consciously applied in daily life. He used the example of biblical characters to reveal the dignity of even the most lowly tasks. He was a particular champion of young working-class women.

Companion, and *Frank Leslie's New York Journal* were among the "penny dreadfuls" that paid for "blood-and-thunder" tales. Though they paid very little—five or six dollars at first and later twenty-five dollars—they now amounted to a steady source of income Louisa could count on. Her biggest coup was the publication of a short story in a new prestigious magazine, the *Atlantic Monthly,* which was edited by the great literary celebrity James Russell Lowell. To Louisa's stagestruck delight, one of her plays, *Nat Bachelor's Pleasure Trip,* was also performed in a small Boston theater in 1860. She was finally confident enough to begin work on her first long novel. It was called, simply, *Moods,* and was inspired by a line from Emerson, whom she revered: "Life is a train of moods like a string of beads; and as we pass through them they prove to be many colored lenses, which paint the world their own hue, and each shows us only what lies in its own focus." The story was a cautionary tale about a young woman who foolishly decides to marry for the wrong reasons. Back in the attic at Orchard House, which had become her favorite writing spot, Louisa recounted:

> From the 2nd to the 25th [February 1861] I sat writing, with a run at dusk; could not sleep, & for three days was so full of it I could not stop to get up. Mother made me a green silk cap with a red bow, to match the old green and red party wrap, which I wore as a "glory cloak." Thus arrayed I sat in groves of manuscripts....I didn't care if the world returned to chaos if I & my inkstand only "lit" in the same place.

She was so caught up in her first great work that she did not realize that chaos *was* coming. It would take the form of a bloody and violent civil war that would profoundly change her life as well as the lives of millions of other Americans.

The Alcott family had long been a part of the Underground Railroad. They had sheltered and hidden at least one fugitive slave en route to Canada as early as 1847. They had publicly protested the Compromise of 1850, which paved the way for California's admission as a free state but opened the territories gained after the Mexican War to slavery, and the Kansas–Nebraska Act of 1854, which overturned the old Missouri Compromise forbidding slavery in either of these future states. And they helped organize public meetings to hear firsthand accounts of the horrors of slavery by escaped slaves like Harriet Tubman and Frederick Douglass. But neither the Alcotts nor anyone else could have foreseen that on April 12, 1861, the commander of the army of the newly formed Confederate States of America would fire upon the Union stronghold at Fort Sumter in South Carolina or that this would be the opening act in a four-year tragedy, the likes of which the nation had never seen.

As a feverent abolitionist, Louisa longed to join the parade of men trooping off to war, but she had to be content at Orchard House picking lint, rolling bandages, sewing uniforms, and working on her novel. To add to her restlessness, when she finally finished *Moods*, she could find no publisher. The war meant hard times even for the most illustrious authors. So she resumed writing short stories. The new editor at the *Atlantic Monthly* rejected her submissions to him with the curt message, "Tell Louisa to stick to her teaching. She can never write." She was demoralized by this harsh judgment. "The accumulation of her disappointments and failures had worn her down to the last grain at last." She tried a serious course of reading, hoping for something to take her mind off her troubles. One day, she came across Florence Nightingale's recently published *Notes on Nursing*. Up until that time, nursing had been a male profession and was neither respectable nor organized. But Nurse Nightingale's clean and orderly front-line hospitals had saved the lives of thousands of wounded soldiers during the Crimean War (1854–1856), in which England, France, Turkey, and Sardinia fought against Russia. Louisa, "fixed on a life of striving," had finally found her true vocation. She announced the news to her family with a mixture of joy and relief: She would volunteer as a nurse in the Union army.

November 29, 1862

Louisa wrote in her journal: "Thirty years old today. The official age of spinsterhood, but no matter. Decided to go to Washington as a nurse if I could find a place. Help needed, & I love nursing & must let out my pent-up energy in some new way. Winter is always a hard and dull time, & if I am away there is one less to feed and warm and worry over."

The family turned out to see her off at the Concord depot on a cold, wet morning in early December. Her father, looking tall, handsome, and a bit forlorn, said, "It seems I am sending my only 'son' off to war. Be a valiant little soldier, my dear."

"And try to get some rest each day," her mother added with her customary solicitude and a warm hug. "You know how ragged you get, Louy, when you work for hours on end. You must think of yourself now and then and try to be moderate in all things, even your devotion to your patients."

Young May pleaded excitedly, "Do write and tell us of all your most lurid adventures, Louy!"

Anna and John, who were expecting their first child in a few months, were more sedate in their farewells, but their emotions were betrayed by tears. Louisa felt a suspicious amount of moisture well up in her own hazel-blue eyes, but she resolutely ignored it. She had to focus on what lay ahead and think about her precious "dear ones" later. Once she reached Boston, she would have to try to secure a railpass to Washington, D.C., where she had been assigned with barely twenty-four hours' notice. She felt a growing sense of the enormity of the task she had undertaken. She was about to leave the only world she had ever known, and she suspected that the new one she was entering would demand all her courage and fortitude.

When she finally reached the nation's capital, it was late at night, too late for the sightseeing she desperately wanted to do. But there was a constant stream of wagon traffic, and the brightly lit warehouses that surrounded the sprawling railyard seemed to be hives of activity, even at this hour. From the window of the hackney cab she hired, Louisa caught the merest glimpse of the imposing Capitol building. Then she saw the White House along Pennsylvania Avenue. To her surprise, the lamps were still burning in one wing, and carriages were rolling in and out of the great iron gate. Perhaps President Lincoln was meeting with his generals and planning military strategy. This was not sleepy Concord where every citizen was abed soon after sundown; this was a place where momentous events appeared to be happening! The thought sent a shiver of excitement down her spine.

A short while later, the cab driver deposited her without ceremony on the rickety steps of the old and rather dilapidated Union Hotel, which had been rechristened the Union Hotel Hospital. A guard was posted at the door, and she feared that she would have to produce some special pass or countersign, but he simply nodded and pulled the doorbell to announce her arrival. A gray-clad nurse materialized and led her upstairs to the old servants' quarters. There were so many women assigned to the room where Louisa was supposed to sleep that she had to leave her trunk outside and she barely managed to squeeze her full skirts through the narrow spaces between the bedsteads. She was so tired that the lumpy, evil-smelling mattress onto which she collapsed seemed like heaven. She fell asleep without the usual

*insomnia that plagued her and rested soundly until a half
hour before sunrise, when one of her new roommates shook
her shoulder and said, not unkindly, "Time to get up, sleepy-
head. You're on duty in ten minutes."*

*Louisa, sat up, rubbed her eyes, and struggled into the
shapeless smock she had been given. It was a good thing
she had been too tired to undress when she arrived. She
had only a few minutes to down a washy mug of coffee in
the canteen before she was led to one of the makeshift
wards in the grand ballroom on the first floor. Later, she
would write of that first awful day, "I began my new life
by seeing a poor man die at dawn and sitting all day
between a boy with pneumonia and a man shot through
the lungs. A strange day, but I did my best; and when I put
my mother's little black shawl around the boy while he sat
up panting for breath, he smiled and said, 'You are really
motherly, ma'am.' I felt as if I was getting on....The suffering round me made me long to comfort everyone."*

*She was a quick learner, and she learned to put her
"bashfulness in her pocket" as she cared for her patients.
She had the tenderest of touches, and she knew the value
of a warm smile to young men who were not only injured
in body but in spirit, and who missed their mothers,
wives, and sisters faraway at home. Louisa herself was
over five hundred miles from home, alone among
strangers, performing painful duties all day long, and leading a life of constant fatigue and worry among hundreds
of men and boys in all stages of suffering, disease, and
death. But she had no regrets. For the first time, she felt
that her existence really mattered. She rose at five or six
o'clock every morning, dressed by lamplight, and ran
through the ward throwing up the window sashes. The
soldiers grumbled and shivered, but she told them quite
sternly, and quite correctly, that the air inside the hospital*

was bad enough to breed pestilence. Next, she poked up the fire and distributed extra blankets. Then, she tried to ignore the cold, the damp, the dirt, and the vile odors as she inspected and changed dressings, adjusted pillows, held drinking cups, emptied bedpans, and told jokes to distract herself as well as her patients. Sometimes she would take a break for a hasty meal that never varied: rancid beef, mealy bread, and greasy butter. In the evenings, until she was relieved by a night nurse at nine o'clock, she read books and newspapers aloud to the whole ward and wrote letters home for those men who were too ill to do so themselves, or, saddest of all, who were dying.

Her favorite, whom she called the "prince of patients," was a young man just her age named John. He was a Virginia blacksmith. Although John would be labeled a common man, it was Louisa's opinion that he was all that anyone could expect or ask for in the first gentleman in the land. Under his plain speech and unpolished manner, she saw a "noble character, a heart as warm and tender as a woman's, a nature as frank and fresh as any child's." He was tall, handsome, mortally wounded, and dying royally, without reproach, repining, or remorse. She grieved that he would not have the chance to make his mark on the world, but she knew that his influence upon the other patients in the ward was as important and as lasting a legacy as any man could offer. She wrote in her journal that he proved beyond any doubt "that real goodness is never wasted."

The morning that John died, Louisa was sitting beside him. He held her hand tightly. He uttered no word of complaint, though his wounds were excruciating. His only concern was to make sure his family received his last letter before the official notification of his death came through. When he breathed his last, his grip did not loosen, and Louisa did not draw away her hand. When she finally

*tried, she could not, and one of the other patients had to
assist her. She had never been so devastated. A part of her
died then and there for John, and for all those brave young
men just like him. Then she stood up, drew a long, shuddering breath, pulled the covers over his face, and called
for the orderlies to take his body to the morgue, for the
bed was needed right away.*

LOUISA ARRIVED AT THE UNION HOTEL HOSPITAL the day
before the disastrous Federal defeat at Fredericksburg. The carnage was terrible. Wounded arrived by the wagonload. The relatively sheltered, inexperienced young woman had no idea what
horrors lay in store. She had brought parlor games to entertain;
she ended up "reeling off pages and pages of *David Copperfield*
from memory to a man who was having his arm taken off without ether." Although soldiers, at the very least, were put through
a minimum of training, one biographer noted that nurses were
sent without any warning into an inferno. Louisa was under-
standably shocked by the sight of blood and gore in surgery and
by the agony of the wounded, but she steeled herself, and soon
after her arrival, she asked to assist in harrowing procedures that
even veteran nurses tried to avoid. She volunteered, unsuccessfully, for a transfer to a front-line hospital. But what never ceased
to disturb her was the disorganization and incompetence of the
hospital staff. One of the doctors whom she routinely assisted
drank so heavily that his hands trembled in the operating room.
Another was timid and "fearfully slow." The nurses were an ill-
mannered, ill-tempered, and ill-trained lot more interested in
wages and free room and board than in emulating Florence
Nightingale. In the opinion of the matron, Hannah Ropes, most
of them could barely "keep the patients from falling out of bed."

By contrast, "Sister Alcott" seemed like a godsend. She took
on every task, no matter how revolting or difficult, with a quiet

good humor. She never complained, never shirked, never gossiped. She made a real difference throughout the entire hospital. But in January, she, the matron, and dozens of patients contracted typhoid pneumonia. Many, including Hannah Ropes, died almost immediately. It was feared that Louisa would die, too, if something were not done quickly. She was weak and delirious. Her father was sent for, and he rushed her home to Orchard House. She lay near death for three weeks. She lost so much weight that she began to look like a skeleton with feverish, empty eyes. Her one vanity, her lovely chestnut hair—all one and a half yards of it—was shorn. Her parents recalled how Lizzie had been at the end; it seemed likely that Louisa would share her tragic fate. But then she rallied. Just as she could not take the fatal plunge into the Concord River when she was filled with despair, she could not give up now.

When she was on her feet again, Louisa appeared to have recovered fully from her ordeal. In truth, however, her health was permanently marred. The war had done as much to her in a few months "as it had done in four years to some others." She herself said, "I was never ill before and never well afterwards." After her convalescence, she wrote a long story called *Hospital Sketches*. It was published in four installments in *Commonwealth* magazine and as a book in 1863. Here is an excerpt that reveals how much of her own experience is thinly disguised. The narrator is a young woman named Nurse Periwinkle:

There they were! "our brave boys," as the papers justly call them, for cowards could hardly have been so riddled with shot and shell, so torn and shattered, nor have borne suffering for which we have no name, with an uncomplaining fortitude, which made one glad to cherish each as a brother. In they came, some on stretchers, some in men's arms, some feebly staggering along propped on rude crutches, and one lay stark and still with covered face, as a comrade gave his name to be recorded before they carried him away to the dead-house. All was hurry and confusion; the hall was full of these wrecks of humanity, for the most exhausted could not reach a bed till duly ticketed and registered; the walls were lined with rows of such as could sit, the floor covered with more disabled, the steps and doorways filled with helpers and lookers-on; the sound of many feet and voices made that usually quiet hour as noisy as noon; and in the midst of it all, the matron's face brought more comfort to many a poor soul than the cordial draughts she administered, or the cheery words that welcomed all, making of the hospital a home.

The sight of several stretchers, each with its legless, armless, or desperately wounded occupant, entering my ward, admonished me that I was there to work, not to wonder or to weep; so I corked up my feelings and returned to the path of duty, which was rather "a hard road to travel" just then....

Curious contrast of the tragic and comic met one everywhere; and some touching as well as ludicrous episodes might have been recorded that day. A six-foot New Hampshire man, with a leg broken and perforated by a piece of shell so large that, had I not seen the wound, I should have regarded the story as a Munchausenism [a lie or exaggeration], beckoned me to come and help him, as he could not sit up, and both his bed and his beard were getting plentifully annointed with soup. As I fed my big nestling with corresponding mouthfuls, I asked him how he felt during the battle.

"Well, 'twas my fust, you see, so I ain't ashamed to say that I was a trifle flustered in the beginnin', there was such an all-fired racket; for ef there's anything I do spleen agin, it's noise. But when my mate, Eph Sylvester, caved, with a bullet through his head, I got mad, and pitched in licketty cut...."

Observing that the man next to him had left his meal untouched, I offered the same service I had performed for his neighbor, but he shook his head.

"Thank you, ma'am; I don't think I'll ever eat again, for I'm shot in the stomach. But I'd like a drink of water if you ain't busy."

I rushed away, but the water-pails were gone to be refilled, and it was some time before they reappeared. I did not forget my first patient, meanwhile, and with the first mugful, hurried back to him. He seemed asleep; but something in the tired white face caused me to listen at his lips for a breath. None came. I touched his forehead; it was cold: and then I knew that, while he waited, a better nurse than I had given him a cooler draught, and healed him with a touch. I laid the sheet over the quiet sleeper, whom no noise could now disturb; and, half an hour later, the bed was empty. It seemed a poor requital for all he had sacrificed and suf-fered,—that hospital bed, lonely even in a crowd; for there was no familiar face for him to look his last upon; no friendly voice to say, Good-bye; no hand to lead him gently down into the Valley of the Shadow; and he vanished, like a drop in that red sea upon whose shores so many women stand lamenting. For a moment I felt bitterly indignant at this seeming carelessness of the value of life, the sanctity of death; then consoled myself with the thought that, when the great muster roll was called, these nameless men might be promoted above the many whose tall monuments record the barren honors they have won.

Hospital Sketches was an immediate success when it appeared. There had been few accounts of the war that were so realistic, so vivid, or so compelling. And none were written by women. Louisa effectively captured the spirit of the ordinary rank-and-file soldier, and she had the ingenious notion of letting him speak for himself in his own distinct dialect. The enthusiastic public reception for the book led the author to reflect with some bemusement,

A year ago I had no publisher & went begging my wares, now *three* have asked me for something....There is a sudden hoist for a meek and lowly scribbler who was told to "stick to her teaching," & never had a literary friend to lend a helping hand! Fifteen years of hard grubbing may be coming to an end after all, & I may yet "pay all the debts, fix the house, send May to Italy & keep the old folks cosy," as I've said I would so long yet so hopelessly.

JUST AFTER LINCOLN'S REELECTION in 1864, Louisa submitted
Moods to another publisher, and it was accepted. The initial printing sold out during the first week. There was great rejoicing in the
Alcott household. Louisa was on her way to achieving fame and
fortune. She was invited to dine with the literary lions of Boston,
and she could even afford a few modest gowns in which to appear.
Then, several prominent critics decided to publish unfavorable
reviews, and the second printing collected dust on the shelves. Fame
and fortune did not materialize after all, and once again, Louisa was
forced to fall back on writing potboilers under assumed names.

A few months after the Confederate surrender at Appomattox,
she was invited to travel to Europe as a companion and nurse for a
young invalid, Anna Weld. Should she go? The characteristically
decisive Louisa was so uncertain that she did not give her answer
until the evening before the ship sailed. On the one hand, she
longed to fulfill her old dream of exploring far-off places. On the
other, she was afraid her family could not do without her. Finally,
her adventurous spirit prevailed, and the old traveling trunk was
hauled down out of the rafters of the barn in Concord. With her
charge, Louisa toured one grand city after another: London,
Brussels, Paris, Cologne, Frankfurt, Heidelberg, Geneva, and
Nice among them. Always powerfully affected by her surround-
ings, "Each carved statue, tiled roof, beautiful view set her blood
pounding; each historical memory made her pulse beat faster." In
Switzerland, she struck up a friendship with a handsome and
lively musician, Ladislas Wisniewski, an exiled veteran of the
Polish nationalist revolution of 1863. He and Louisa grew close.
Based on certain allusions in her journal, some biographers spec-
ulate that he may have even proposed to her; others claim his true
affection was for Anna Weld. Whatever the relationship, it is
indisputable that Ladislas and Louisa shared a special bond of
affection that was preserved through correspondence for many
years afterward. (And the young Pole would be one of several
inspirations for the character, Laurie, in *Little Women*.)

Eventually, Louisa resigned her position and went back to London on her own. She attended sessions of Parliament, listened to speeches by such rising political figures as John Stuart Mill, and met a number of influential social reformers. She sold the English rights to *Moods* to a London publisher and then sailed for home after a nearly year-long absence. She had broadened her perspective of the world, but, even more important, she had gained a new appreciation of her homeland and a new measure of self-confidence. She arrived in Concord just in time, too; as she feared, the Alcotts had not been able to manage without her and were once again on the verge of financial ruin.

May 1868

Perched precariously on the attic window sill at Orchard House, Louisa could see what were surely three of the fabled seven wonders of the world: a green and gold checkered hayfield that seemed to run on for miles under a brilliant blue sky; a thick grove of century-old locusts, maples, and oaks that cast a shadow as cool and dark as midnight; and an old weathered and sagging barn that had been transformed by her imagination countless times into a castle fortress high on a mountaintop, a treasure ship lost in a stormy sea, and a magical island paradise populated by wild beasts and cannibals. She let her glance linger on this last sight for some moments. The barn was where on rainy afternoons she, Anna, Lizzie, and May had romped and polished their acting skills with plenty of speechifying, sword-play, and feats of derring-do. Many a good time they had enjoyed in that place, even though they were poor as church mice.

Louisa jumped off the sill and carelessly dusted her hands off on her skirts. Thank goodness she was back where she belonged, in good old sleepy Concord where not one truly exciting thing had happened since some pesky, upstart revolutionaries had fired a "shot heard round the world." And that had been all of ninety years ago. Traveling to Europe had been a wonderful cure for her depression after the war and the poor reception of Moods, but now it was time to put the past—for good or ill— behind her and write something that would set the literary world on fire. Her family was depending on her. She simply had to come up with a brilliant idea. Unfortunately, the harder she tried, the more brilliance eluded her. Dozens of ideas sprang to mind, but none of them were much more than satisfactory and some were downright awful. Finally, after weeks of waiting futilely for an idea to appear like a rescue ship on the horizon, she decided to produce, as a purely temporary expedient, something that had been suggested to her almost a year earlier by Thomas Niles, a Boston publisher. It was to be a novel specifically written for young girls—there was nothing like it on the market, nor had there ever been, he said. Louisa declined, protesting that she knew nothing about the creatures except, of course, for what she had gleaned from her own and her sisters' experiences. But now she desperately needed money, so she welcomed the notion. She sat down at the her desk and stared at the blank white foolscap waiting to be filled, line by line, page by page, with her untidy scrawl. Really, perhaps she should just go downstairs for a bit and see if any help was needed in the kitchen. She hated cooking, but.... "No," *she told herself sternly.* "It's time to begin. After all, you silly goosecap, for the past ten years you've been telling anyone who would listen that you intended to write about your own family some day. Well, this is the perfect opportunity." *Without further hesitation, she picked up her pen, dipped it in the inkwell, and suddenly the words began to flow:*

"Christmas won't be Christmas without any presents," grumbled Jo, lying on the rug.

"It's so dreadful to be poor!" sighed Meg, looking down at her old dress.

"I don't think it's fair for some girls to have lots of pretty things, and other girls to have nothing at all," added Amy, with an injured sniff.

"We've got father and mother, and each other, anyhow," said Beth, contentedly, from her corner....

Louisa wrote, and wrote, and wrote. She wrote until her fingers ached, and she had to put one arm—the lame one that had never really gotten better since her bout with typhoid—in a sling. Her head ached terribly too; she fancied it might even explode. Still, she wrote. Her mother appeared at about seven o'clock with a lamp and a plate of cucumber sandwiches. She set them down without a word, knowing that when her daughter was caught up in a story she would barely heed anything else. Abba was right; Louisa didn't even notice the light, and the sandwiches remained untouched. She was writing when the sun came up again. About mid-morning, she stopped for a few hours' rest before she was up and at work again. She wrote feverishly, as if in a delirium. Occasionally as the spring days gave way to summer, she would sleep, eat, and pretend to converse intelligently with her family. From time to time, Abba would climb the stairs and peek around the door to whisper gently, "Does genius burn?" or "May I get you a glass of barley water and some sweet biscuits?" Her father would leave silent tributes on her desk—a basket of ripe, red apples or a bunch of wildflowers that gave a fresh scent to the musty air of the attic. But most of the time, Louisa was alone in a world of her own making.

When she finally descended in the middle of July to "resume her acquaintance with the living," she had written over four hundred pages about four young sisters who live in Civil War-era New England. They are poor but well educated. Their father is a chaplain in the Union army, their mother is a good samaritan who not only takes care of others in the community but also teaches her daughters how to be generous and giving. Each daughter learns this lesson in a different, sometimes painful, way.

The manuscript was duly shipped off to the publisher. He was of the opinion that it was rather dull and uninteresting. He stalled for some weeks and then finally offered to buy it in August. The amount she would be paid was modest, but she would be allowed to retain the copyright (which had never happened before), so Louisa immediately agreed. In October, Little Women *appeared. The phrase was borrowed from Bronson Alcott, who had often used it to refer to his four daughters when they were children. After scanning the finished text, the author judged, "It reads better than I expected. Not a bit sensational, but simple and true, for we really lived most of it; and if it succeeds that will be the reason of it. Mr. Niles likes it better now, and says some of the girls who have read it say it is 'splendid!' As it is for them, they are the best critics, so I should be satisfied."*

IN ORDER TO RESCUE the family from debt, Louisa wrote twenty-five stories in the year after she returned from Europe. She literally worked herself into a serious illness. She suffered from rheumatism, a painful nerve disease known as "neuralgia," and a mysterious ailment her doctors couldn't diagnose but that is now identified as mercury poisoning.[8] When the pain became too

---

8   During the Civil War, Louisa and thousands of other typhoid victims were given massive doses of calomel, a drug that has since been proven to cause mercury poisoning.

much to bear, she tried various cures, including dangerous opiates, which were very much in vogue at the time. In 1868, she landed the editorship of a popular children's magazine, *Merry's Museum,* which allowed her to leave story writing for a time and work on *Little Women.* She may have judged the book to be "not a bit sensational" in the literary sense, but it turned out to be an overnight sensation. Part I, which she wrote in May through July, came out on October 1, and received rave reviews.[9] A second printing was ordered almost immediately, and it was followed by a third and a fourth. Louisa paid off the family's bills and loans, some of which had been outstanding for a decade or more, but she had hardly any time to enjoy her newfound prosperity. Within a month, she was hard at work on Part II, which was completed on New Year's Day and published on April 14, 1869. Her publisher was no doubt pleased to learn that only a month later the transcontinental railroad would be opened, for this meant that the second volume would be the first novel ever read simultaneously on both coasts.

It would be difficult to exaggerate the impact of *Little Women* on American society. Louisa became one of the most important authors of her day. *Little Women* gained hundreds of thousands of readers during her lifetime; millions have read and continue to read it since. A modest little story—intended merely for the entertainment and moral instruction of adolescent females, written by an obscure New England spinster who didn't want to write it at all—has become a book for the ages. Of course, critics have always been loath to admit that it belongs in the canon of great Western literature. *Little Women* seems "too simple, too sweet." But, as a defender of its true merit argues, "Underneath is a truth almost severe." The situations and characters are neither one-dimensional, sentimental creations nor typical juvenile fare. Louisa was

---

9   Today, virtually every edition of *Little Women* is published as one volume, but when it originally appeared, readers had to wait an entire year to learn what happened to the young March sisters.

surrounded by Transcendentalists like her father, Emerson, and Thoreau, who liked to deal in the abstract, but "she was herself a realist of the first order." She wrote with "courageous candor" about the Marches who were modeled on the real-life Alcott sisters: "Meg," who was Anna; "Beth," who was Lizzie; "Amy," who was May; and "Jo," who was Louisa. Louisa would write tellingly, "All is fish that comes into the literary net....I turn my adventures into bread and butter." After Lizzie's death, she added, "I feel as if I could write better now,— more truly of the things I have felt and therefore know." And around the time *Little Women* appeared, she declared that "the nearer I keep to nature the better the work is."

Little Women—intended merely for the entertainment and moral instruction of adolescent females, written by an obscure New England spinster who didn't want to write it at all—has become a book for the ages.

The characters in *Little Women* have serious faults as well as virtues; they are not plaster saints. They struggle, just as Christian did in John Bunyan's classic Christian apology *Pilgrim's Progress,* with burdens of sin. Meg is materialistic and vain. Amy is spoiled and selfish. Beth is unassertive and lacks courage. Jo, who is deliberately presented in the least flattering terms of all, is temperamental, moody, impatient, stubborn, and full of pride. But she is also the most lovable of the sisters, for she is brimming with high spirits, dauntless courage, and romantic idealism. She performs the most impulsive—and outrageous—acts of kindness without a thought for her own interests. She is "alive" in a way few heroines ever written about are. They are "just children," as the saying goes, but the March sisters are also characters to whom adults can relate. As an early critic once observed,

> Youth is a period of life which deserves much more consideration than it often receives. It is the integrating period during which we make our characters and form those habits of thought and action which mainly determine our destiny. The bloom of youth may

conceal this internal conflict, but it is there nonetheless, and frequently a very severe one. "You have no idea of the trials I have
had," I once heard a school-girl of sixteen say, the perfect picture
of health and happiness; and those who remember well their own
youth will not be inclined to laugh at this. The tragedy of childhood
is the commonest form of tragedy; and youth is a melodrama in
which pathos and humor are equally mingled. Those who by some
chance have escaped this experience and have had the path of early
life made smooth for them, may grow to be thrifty trees but are not
likely to bear much fruit. It is for her clear perception of these conditions and her skill and address in dealing with them that Miss
Alcott deserves the celebrity that is now attached to her name.

Another reviewer said that reading *Little Women* is like unlatch-
ing the door to a strange house and finding that it is as familiar as
one's own. The local is "transmuted into the universal," and thus
the book does not "merely lure children from play and old men
from the chimney corner but shapes character for generations to
come." Incredibly, Louisa managed to achieve all this at the same
time that she "captured the American family" and made "the
domestic novel a part of the life and letters of New England." But
one biographer claims an even more lofty distinction for *Little
Women* by alleging that it is the "first purely American novel.
There had previously been colonial novels, Puritan novels, Indian
novels, Southern novels, and New England novels; but no
American novel had appeared up until then. *Little Women* was
the first novel written that reflected the Union."

Thanks to the tremendous commercial success of *Little
Women*, by the end of the 1860s, Louisa had fulfilled all her
ambitions. She had not only freed her family from poverty but
had become rich and famous. She was a virtual idol to her readers. She could travel anywhere, meet anyone, and buy anything.
If she chose, she could at last marry and live like one of the
heroines she wrote about in her pulp fiction romances. But

success had come too late and at too great a price. Dear Lizzie was gone. In a few short years, three more members of her beloved family would die: her mother, Abba; her sister, May; and Anna's husband, John. Abba's death, after a long and painful decline, was the hardest to bear. She had been the central influence and emotional anchor in Louisa's life. Now, Louisa couldn't seem to rest, and there was no one to remind her to take care of herself in the way that her mother had. She kept on writing. She had worked at such a furious pace for so long that it had become something of an obsession. As a girl, she had given up her freedom to be the "knight errant" for the Alcotts. Now that all the dragons were slain, what on earth was she to do with herself? Even fame proved to be a burden. She was frequently mobbed when she went out in public. Ironically, when she was young she couldn't afford proper gowns; now, she had closets full of them, but they would literally be torn off her back if she dared appear at any large public function.

By the end of the 1860s, Louisa had fulfilled all her ambitions. She had not only freed her family from poverty but had become rich and famous. She was a virtual idol to her readers.

The final blow came when Bronson Alcott died at age eighty-nine after a six-year illness. Louisa nursed him, just as she had nursed Lizzie and Abba, until her own health wouldn't permit it. She could neither sleep nor eat properly by this time. She may have suffered from intestinal cancer. She died in a nursing home in Roxbury, Massachusetts, at age fifty-five on March 6, 1888, which was two days after her father's death.

BUT TO END THE STORY of Louisa May Alcott's life so starkly would not do justice to this indomitable American heroine. After *Little Women* appeared, she wrote such wonderful and widely

---

10 In all, Louisa wrote thirty-five books.

acclaimed books as *Good Wives* (1869); *An Old-Fashioned Girl* (1870); *Little Men* (1871); *Work* (1873); *Eight Cousins* (1875); *Rose in Bloom* (1876); *A Modern Mephistophiles* (1877); *Under the Lilacs* (1878); *Jack and Jill* (1880); and *Jo's Boys* (1886).[10] She also became a dedicated supporter of women's suffrage, prison reform, and private orphanages, schools, and charities. She not only wrote scores of articles trying to educate the public about these issues, she also became actively involved in championing them, even though it meant relinquishing what little privacy she still enjoyed.

Best of all, at age forty-six, Louisa became a mother. Her sister May, who died of complications ensuing from childbirth, had named her older sister guardian of her daughter, Lulu. Louisa was stunned and grateful to receive this "precious legacy." In many ways, the responsibility of caring for a child provided her with a new lease on life. She wrote in her journal, "I see now why I have lived," and she described Lulu as "a happy thing, laughing & waving her hands....My heart is full of pride & joy & the touch of the dear little hands seems to take away the bitterness of grief. I often go at night to see if she is *really* here & the sight of the little yellow head is like sunshine to me."

Louisa's May Alcott's entire life was one in which love and labor were inextricably intertwined. High idealism rather than ambition was her driving motivation. She was fiery. She was gentle. She was brave on behalf of others' interests and timid on behalf of her own. In a sonnet, her father called her "Duty's faithful child." A line she once wrote about her mother could be used to describe her even more aptly: "Life has been so hard for her and she is so brave, so glad to spend herself for others." Her last book, *A Garland for Girls*, was published in 1887. Written from her sickbed, this collection of stories does not hint of despair; instead it expresses "a vigorous sense of the life of her times" and, above all, her blithe spirit. She indirectly referred to this spirit once by saying simply, "I had lots of troubles, so I wrote jolly tales." At age seventeen, she wrote in her journal that her one true desire was to become "a truly good and useful woman." She was all that and more. As a biographer summed it up, "No one equalled her as a teacher of democracy in daily life, of happiness in small things, and of the inspiration in the simple affections." Another said: "Louisa's writing has shown generations of readers who they are gently alongside what they could become, reassuring them that the distance between is only a human step."

SUGGESTED READINGS

The main sources for this chapter were: Cornelia Meigs, *Invincible Louisa* [1933] (Boston: Little, Brown & Co., 1961); Katharine Antony, *Louisa May Alcott* (Westport, CT: Greenwood Press, 1937); Gloria T. Delamar, *Louisa May Alcott and* Little Women (Jefferson, NC: McFarland and Company, 1990); Ruth K. MacDonald, *Louisa May Alcott* (Boston: Twayne Publishers, 1983); Madeleine Stern, *Louisa May Alcott* [1950] (Norman: University of Oklahoma Press, 2d ed. rev., 1971); and Daniel Shealy, Madeleine Stern, and Joel Myerson, eds., *The Journals of Lousia May Alcott* (Boston: Little, Brown & Co., 1989). Although it presents a "politically correct" feminist interpretation and belittles the literary value of *Little Women,* I also found Martha Saxton's *Louisa May Alcott: A Modern Biography* [1977] (New York: Farrar, Straus & Giroux, 1995) to contain valuable new information.

Other novels by Louisa May Alcott are widely available today, but for those who would like to read more of her short fiction, I recommend another book edited by Shealy, Stern, and Myerson, *Lousia May Alcott: Selected Fiction* (Boston: Little, Brown & Co., 1990) and Stern's *Louisa May Alcott Unmasked: Collected Thrillers* (Boston: Northeastern University Press, 1995).

George Washington Carver

Scientist and Educator

(c. 1864–1943)

I love to think of nature as an unlimited broadcast-ing station, through which God speaks to us every hour, if only we will tune in.

—George Washington Carver

January 1865

In the Ozark mountains of Missouri the winter wind wailed like a banshee, rattling the doors and windows of the little one-room cabin that belonged to Moses and Susan Carver. Susan paced in front of the fire whispering over and over again, "Oh, whatever have they done with them?" Moses was restless too, but he stayed put in his rocker, gripping the arms with his deformed hands. He knew what "they," the Confederate guerrillas, were capable of doing. A few years back, they tortured him in order to find a cache of money they suspected he had hidden. First, they hung him from a walnut tree by his thumbs. Then, they burned his feet with hot coals. He still bore the scars, but the stubborn German immigrant farmer had the grim satisfaction of knowing that he had won the battle of wills; he hadn't told them a blessed thing. But the very same soldiers had recently returned, and this time they took something more precious than gold—the "they" that Susan was whispering about—the slave girl, Mary, and her one-year-old son, George. Only Mary's three-year-old, Jim, had been spared, and that was because Moses had managed to hide him in the woods.

The Carvers, like many westerners, were opposed to the institution of slavery. When a neighbor brought the news that President Lincoln had issued the Emancipation Proclamation in 1863, Moses was so delighted that he grabbed his wife and danced a jig. Mary gathered her young sons in her arms and wept tears of joy. But then the neighbor told them that the decree applied only to states "in open rebellion." So slavery was still legal in Missouri.[1] They all grew quiet and solemn at this news.

---

[1] Slavery continued in Missouri until a new state constitution took effect on July 4, 1865.

Susan put her arm around Mary and said comfortingly, "Ach, don't worry. Surely it will only be a little while longer until the war is over and you are free." The Carvers were afraid to act on their own initiative. The times were dangerous and uncertain. So, they protected Mary and her children by keeping them as slaves while giving them a cabin of their own and treating them like family. When Mary and George were kidnapped, they posted a reward and fretted as if their own blood kin had been taken.

Suddenly, on this stormy winter night, there was a loud pounding on the cabin door. Susan ran to open it, ignoring Mose's warning that it might be another raid. A big, roughly dressed man carrying an awkward blanket-covered bundle in his arms filled the doorway.

"Come in! Come in!" Susan waved him in.

"What have you got there, Bentley?" Moses addressed the man eagerly.

"Why, this here's the child you was lookin' for. I weren't able to find his mama, even though I tracked the bushwhackers who took her all the way to Arkansas. I doubt anyone will ever find her."

Susan took the bundle and peeked inside. It was George, sure enough. He was small and appeared pale despite his dark skin. His puny arms and legs were like matchsticks, and he seemed to struggle for every breath.

"It's whooping cough, and he's got it bad," Bentley said gruffly. "I doubt the poor mite will make it through the night. Still, I brought him back, and I'm entitled to some reward." He shifted his weight from one foot to the other like a guilty schoolboy, embarrassed to be asking.

"I have got a fine race horse tucked away in a corral down in the woods south of here," Moses said easily enough. "I have kept him safe from the Johnny Rebs all this

while, and he is worth three hundred dollars. You are welcome to him." He was so glad to have George back that he would have given twice that amount, even though he had a well-deserved reputation for *"being tight with his money."*

Susan murmured as she hugged the sleeping infant, *"Won't anything bad happen to you from now on. You are not only going to live, my little one, you are going to surprise them all and grow up to be mighty special."*

George must have sensed her meaning, for his eyes opened wide at this declaration, spoken with so much confidence. They did not appear weak like the rest of his body. They were bright and alert. He would live, and perhaps he would surprise them all, just as the old woman prophesied.

GEORGE WASHINGTON CARVER was born near Diamond, Missouri, sometime between 1860 and 1865. Few reliable records exist regarding birthdates for slaves in the mid-nineteenth century, but George himself thought that he was probably born in January of 1864. The Carvers bought his mother, Mary, from a neighbor in 1855 when she was only thirteen years old. In 1859, she bore a son, Jim. Jim and George's father was reputed to be "Big George," a slave on a neighboring farm. Slave marriages were illegal, and he died in a logging accident just after George was born, so no one knows for sure. Mary was never found after being carried off by Confederate raiders, so she was presumed dead. "As a child," says one of his biographers, George "pestered Susan to tell him about his mother, but he learned very little because she always started to cry when she talked of Mary. He frequently stood by Mary's old spinning wheel, as if trying to feel the presence of the woman he could not remember. The spinning wheel and the bill of sale for Mary became two of his most prized possessions as an old man."

Young Jim, who was strong and robust, grew up to be the "hired man" on the Carver farm and received wages for his labor. George, by contrast, was "a frail and sickly child." Bouts of whooping cough and croup had strained his vocal chords and he may have even had tuberculosis. Because he could not manage heavy labor, he was given mainly household chores. This left him with plenty of time for his favorite activity, which was combing the woods for rocks, insects, reptiles, and small animals. He had a secret hiding place in his room for this "collection"—that is, until Susan found out and demanded that he keep it outdoors. Given to terrible stammering, he was quiet and shy around other children and seldom joined any games except mumblety peg or marbles. But his kindness and gentleness earned him many lifelong friends. From an early age, he also displayed unusual talents. "His curiosity seemed to run deeper than average and he quickly mastered whatever was taught him—from the alphabet to crocheting and music." After Susan gave him Louisa May Alcott's *Little Women* to read, he said to himself, "Why, I can do that!" and promptly wrote a "novel" of his own. Most of all, though, George loved learning about Nature. He later reminisced, "I wanted to know the name of every stone and flower and insect and bird and beast. I wanted to know where it got its color, where it got its life—but there was no one to tell me."

Fortunately, there *were* people around who were able to teach him important lessons in life. His adoptive parents, for example, taught him that his character was more important than the color of his skin. In addition, Susan taught him valuable domestic skills that he would use to support himself through many lean years, and Moses taught him to hate waste and to be a competent farmer. And the circuit-riding preachers who appeared at the Locust Grove Church taught him tolerance for different views as well as different denominations. At first, George and Jim were allowed to attend the white school that was held on weekdays in the church, but it was not long before a few bigots in the congregation denied them admission. It was the boys' first direct encounter with racism, and it left them feeling bewildered, ashamed, and afraid.

A year later, in 1877, the Carvers allowed George to move eight miles away to Neosho, where there was a new school for blacks. With his possessions tied up in an old bandanna, the thirteen-year-old walked all the way there by himself. He had no idea where he would live or how he would get by. But, as luck would have it, on his second day he met a kindly black couple who took him in. The woman was a midwife, and she taught George all she knew about healing herbs and folk remedies. She also introduced him to the African Methodist Episcopal Church. In return, George worked hard to earn his keep. He even ran home at recess to help with chores. But he soon found that the education he was getting in Neosho was unsatisfactory because the schoolmaster knew very little. So he hitched a ride on a wagon train that was going to Fort Scott, Kansas, where many blacks were migrating in search of new opportunities. It had been hard to say good-bye to his family, but he had felt an irresistible urge to move on and see new territory. He could not know then that he would never see his brother again; Jim would die in a smallpox epidemic in 1883 at age twenty-four.[2]

Once he arrived in Fort Scott, George moved in with a blacksmith and did the cooking while learning the smithy trade. He also worked part-time in a hotel laundry and in a general store. On the night of March 26, 1879, he and a crowd of one thousand other citizens watched a masked mob lynch a black man in the town square. The victim was beaten, hung from a lamppost, and burned in a bonfire. George was horror-struck. The man was accused of a terrible crime, but nothing could justify this kind of vigilantism.

---

[2]   He visited Moses and Susan about a year after Jim's death, but did not return again to Missouri until Moses was widowed and nearing his one hundredth birthday in 1908.

He packed his bags and fled to another town. At age fifteen, he entered school again and moved in with another black family to work for his room and board. He also began to teach Sunday School at a Methodist church. After a time, he moved on to Minneapolis, Kansas, and operated his own laundry business for several years in a poor district called, appropriately enough, "Poverty Gulch." He enrolled in an all-white school this time and joined the Presbyterian church. In his few spare hours, he read books on medicine and other subjects lent to him by a friendly doctor. Then, he moved yet again to Kansas City, bought a type-writer, and become a depot clerk for the railroad. He was like the proverbial rolling stone, but, with each new move and each new set of experiences, he was learning to become more and more resourceful and independent. In August of 1886, brimming with confidence, he decided to purchase some land and make his fortune as a farmer on the sod house frontier.

July 1887

George sat back on his bare, unshod heels and surveyed the pitiable scene. Dust, dust, and more dust. Even the air was filled with swirling dust devils, making it difficult to see or breathe. He just couldn't understand it. There had been no rain for weeks. The corn he had carefully tended all spring was withering on the stalk, and the vegetables were in even worse shape. He had thought that the winters on the Kansas prairie were bad enough— blinding blizzards that piled up drifts higher than the rooftop, nothing but buffalo and cow dung for fuel, and not a soul to talk to for weeks on end—but, after bitter experience, he now knew the summers were even worse. The sun literally scorched the earth, turning it from a rich, fertile brown to a dull, lifeless gray. The wind was even more merciless; it blew precious seeds and topsoil clean away. *And there wasn't a tree or a bush to provide shade for miles. Instead of a cabin, he had been forced to build a tiny, dark, and dank sod house, so called because it was made of cut and dried strips of turf, on his 160-acre claim south of Beeler, Kansas. In August of 1886, he had spent all his savings on the down payment for the land, a cookstove, some seeds, and his only farming equipment: a spade, a hoe, and a corn planter. He had built his own bed, cupboard, table, and chairs from wood he scavenged in town. His only other worldly wealth consisted of some tattered books, a silver pocket watch, and an old accordion he used to play at school recitals.*

It was ironic that George was faced with almost certain failure as a farmer. Back in Missouri, folks had always called him the Plant Doctor. Even as a young boy, he seemed to know all about sickly plants, and the neighbors often brought him "patients." He loved to nurse them back to health by planting them in the right soil and giving them special care. It was a passion of his, just like sketching. With ink made from berries, roots, and bark, he had made intricate drawings of vegetation, flowers, and trees on scraps of wood, flat pieces of stone, or whatever was handy. Occasionally, he would draw people too, but it was Nature that really fascinated him.

If only he could sink a well! He had tried countless times, but always came up dry. He had to haul water from a spring nearly a mile away, and then only enough for his personal use. Perhaps it was time to call it quits and go back to school. But then he remembered with some remorse his last attempt. He had applied by mail and been accepted at a small Presbyterian college. He pored over the catalogue with eager anticipation and dreamed of taking all the courses it featured. He showed up on the first day of the new term and presented

*himself at the office of the principal where he was told
that he was ineligible—the place was for Indians only!
George had been turned away from schools before
because of his race, but this was a new and bitter twist.
So, was he to be a failure at everything? He leaped to his
feet and shouted as loud as he could, "No! I won't give
up!" even though he was alone, and there was no one to
hear him. The wind snatched the words away and carried them off across the dusty plains, but it didn't matter.
He had his confidence back. Somehow, he would find a
way to bring in this last crop and finish school.*

FORTUNE SOON SMILED on the young man who was filled with
the determination to succeed. The rains came, and he was able to
harvest most of his crops. The following summer, he paid off what
he owed on his property and went on the road again. In the fall
of 1890, he ended up at Simpson College in Indiananola, Iowa, to
complete his high school degree.[3] George was the only black student, but his classmates at this small Methodist institution treated
him as an equal. They knew his only shelter was an abandoned
shack without furniture and that he lived on a diet of cornmeal
and suet, so sometimes they left little anonymous presents of
food, concert tickets, and money at his door. Once, they even took
up a collection and bought a bed, a table, and some chairs for
him. George later recalled with fond appreciation, "They made
me believe I was a real human being." But he wasn't content to
live on charity. He scrounged for an old cookstove, an iron, and
some tin tubs, and he set up a laundry to support himself.

His main academic interest at Simpson was art. But his
teacher thought this was an impractical career choice for a young
black man who was sure to encounter great prejudice and who

---

3 Most nineteenth-century colleges included a high school curriculum.

had no independent means. Knowing of his "green thumb," she encouraged him to enroll in the agricultural program at Iowa State College in Ames. George resisted at first, but he soon came to accept her advice. He knew that his experience not only as a farmer but as a horticulturist would stand him in good stead. On the prairie, he had built a conservatory for a well-to-do neighbor and stocked it with five hundred plants. He had also spent years experimenting with grafting, fertilization, and cross-breeding techniques. And even though it was hard, at twenty-five, to give up his cherished dream of becoming an artist, George knew he could do more for other blacks by becoming a scientist. He burned with a strong desire to be of service to people who had finally escaped slavery but who were still trapped in poverty.

At Ames, he was once again the only black student, but this time he was not warmly welcomed. On his first day, a group of upperclassmen hurled insults at him. And an administrator informed him that he could not room with other students or even dine with them; he was to take his meals in the basement of the dining hall with the "help." He patiently and politely bore all this abuse, for he sincerely believed in the biblical injunction, "And unto him that smiteth thee on the one cheek, offer also the other; and him that taketh away thy cloak forbid not to take thy coat also." He met unkindness with kindness and intolerance with tolerance. And within a few short months, he was one of the most popular figures on campus. Students who had previously snubbed him asked him to join their clubs. Teachers who feared his abilities would be limited praised him for his outstanding academic work and put him at the head of the class. It was an extraordinary turn of events, but then, George was an extraordinary person.

He studied hard, but he still had to take on odd jobs as a waiter, janitor, and laundryman to pay his way through school. He economized by sewing his own clothes and collecting discarded wrapping paper and pencil stubs for taking notes in class. And somehow he found time for extracurricular activities, too. He was appointed as missionary chairman of the Young Men's Christian Association (YMCA) and as a captain in the school's military division. He helped raise funds for the football team. He played the guitar at public recitals and, in a final triumph over his youthful stammer, learned to give dramatic readings. He also joined the debating society, the German club, and the art club. On the few occasions when he was mistreated because of his race, his friends rallied to his defense, and he actually had to restrain them from retaliation. These same friends were aware of his financial straits; when he refused to exhibit his artwork at a prominent show in Cedar Rapids because of the expense, they marched him into a store, bought him a new suit, and handed him a railway ticket. It was a good thing they did, because his *Yucca and Cactus* was one of the paintings selected to represent the state of Iowa at the World's Columbian Exposition (now known as the World's Fair) in Chicago.

> "I wanted to know the name of every stone and flower and insect and bird and beast. I wanted to know where it got its color, where it got its life—but there was no one to tell me."

AFTER HE GRADUATED in 1894, George was offered a job on the faculty as an assistant botanist. He thus entered the history books as the school's first black graduate and its first black professor. He was put in charge of the greenhouse at the Iowa State Experiment Station, the largest experimental farm in the state. He was also given the opportunity of doing postgraduate work with some of the world's leading agricultural scientists. He plunged into the work with intense enthusiasm and usually worked from early in the morning until late at night, but no matter how tired he was, he always rose before dawn to walk in the woods. He carried a battered old tin can and collected specimens of plants, fungi, and rocks, just as he had when he was a boy on the Carver farm in Missouri. He was thirty years old now, but he never tired of searching for new varieties and identifying known ones.

After graduation, flattering job offers began coming in the mail. He thought about accepting some of them, but the truth was that he was happy in Iowa, where the forests were thick with timber, the fields were fertile, and the cattle were fat and healthy. It was an agriculturist's paradise. It was also a perfect place for George to pursue his most serious research interest, which was mycology. He intended to become a world-renowned authority on fungi and plant diseases. According to his colleagues, he was already off to a promising start. One day, however, George received a letter that would profoundly change his life. It was from Booker T. Washington, the principal of the Tuskegee Normal and Industrial School, better known as the Tuskegee Institute, in Tuskegee, Alabama. George had never met Washington, but he certainly knew who he was. Practically everybody in America knew. He was the famous ex-slave and coal miner-turned-educator who had delivered a speech at the 1895 Atlanta Exposition—the biggest and most momentous public event in the South since the end of the Civil War. That a black was permitted to sit on the same platform with the president of the United States, Grover Cleveland, and to address an audience of thousands of white Southerners was in itself cause for amazement, but it was what Washington said in his speech that was most amazing of all. He began by stating a simple fact: "One-third of the population of the South is of the Negro race." He went on to add, "No enterprise to make life better in the South can succeed if it leaves the Negro out. The fact that the Negro has not been left out here, at this Exposition, will do more to strengthen the friendship of the two races than anything that has happened since the dawn of Negro freedom." Then he told the audience a story:

A ship was many days lost at sea. All its water was gone, the sailors were mad with thirst. Suddenly they sighted a friendly vessel. Immediately a signal was sent from the mast: "Water, water; we die of thirst!"

The answer from the friendly vessel at once came back: "Cast down your bucket where you are!"

The captain could not understand. Were they to drink salt water? He ordered the signal to be sent again: "Water, water; send us water!"

Again the answer came: "Cast down your bucket where you are."

Surely there must be some mistake! A third and a fourth time the answer came back: "Cast down your bucket where you are."

At last the captain heeded the message. He cast down his bucket—and it came up full with fresh, sparkling water from the mouth of the Amazon River.

There are those of my race who think to go to a foreign land to better their condition. There are those who think that it is not very important to make a friend of the southern white man who is their next-door neighbor. To them I would say: Cast down your bucket where you are. Cast it down in making friends in every manly way of the people of all races by whom we are surrounded. Cast it down in farming, in mechanics, in business, in domestic service, and in the professions.

There are those of the white race who also look abroad. They want people of foreign birth to come in and bring prosperity to the South. To them I would repeat what I say to my own race: Cast down your bucket where you are. Cast it down among the eight millions of Negroes who have tilled your fields and cleared your forests. They have built your railroads and your cities. They have brought forth treasures from the bowels of the earth. They have helped make possible this Exposition of the progress of the South. Cast your bucket down among these people. They are the most patient, faithful, law-abiding, unresentful people that the world has seen.

Help them to make the most of themselves. Help them to become useful and intelligent citizens. Help them, and it will pay a thousand percent....

George was able to read the full text of this speech, for it was printed in newspapers across the country. Like millions of other Americans, he was deeply inspired. Washington had put into words the vision George had always had in mind when he thought about helping others. Now, he was being asked to prove his dedication to this vision by coming to Tuskegee to teach poor young black men and women about modern agricultural science. He would have to give up everything: the handsome salary, the prestige, the excellent working conditions, the chance to earn a doctorate in mycology. But it was a call to service George simply could not ignore. So he submitted his resignation, packed up all his specimens, donned his only suit, and boarded the train for Alabama.

He arrived at the Tuskegee Institute in Macon County in October 1896. His title, "Director of the Department of Agricultural Research," was grand enough, but it meant little. The fifteen-year-old school boasted only a few crudely constructed brick buildings. There were no shade trees and no sidewalks. Sewage flowed through open ditches and gave off an awful odor. There were no laboratories and no laboratory equipment. The farm equipment consisted of one plow and a pair of oxen. The "dairy" was a butter churn and a few emaciated milk cows. And all this lay smack in the middle of some of the worst ground George had ever seen—two thousand acres of brushy, steep hills and sharply eroded ravines. The top soil had washed away, and nothing remained but sand and clay. He would later learn that the locals had a name for this land, which had been worn out and depleted by generations of cotton production. They called it "Big Hungry." Principal Washington consoled him by pointing out where a new agricultural building was to be built, thanks to a gift of $10,000 from a foundation started by a Connecticut mill owner, but George's heart sank low. This place was far more barren than anything he'd seen on the Kansas prairie. He was relieved that he had made no long-term commitment. He would stay and teach for a year or two, but that was all. He had a standing invitation to go to Paris to paint and further his scientific studies, and he certainly wasn't going to turn it down and remain in this wasteland.

On the first day that he met with his thirteen students, however, he put on a brave front. He congratulated them for choosing to study agriculture when most of the institute's one thousand students preferred to take other supposedly more lofty subjects. He promised that he would show them that there was dignity in working with one's hands and that farming was a fascinating science that shouldn't be associated with the old plantation system. Indeed, farming, he said, was the key to their future and the South's. His enthusiasm was infectious. The students spent the rest of the day helping him rummage through trash bins and rubbish heaps to come up with equipment for the laboratory he proposed to set up immediately. As one account notes, "Broken bottles with their necks cut off evenly had turned into beakers. And old ink bottle with a wick made of twisted string stuck through a cork served for a Bunsen burner. A chipped teacup did duty as a mortar to crush things in. Fruit jar lids held chemicals. A flat iron stood ready to pound things to powder. Pieces of tin with holes of various sizes punched in them had become sifters for grading soil. Reeds turned into tubes to measure and transfer liquids." George added to this miscellaneous assortment the only real piece of equipment the laboratory would have for several years—a microscope that his former teachers and friends had given him when he left Iowa State.

The makeshift laboratory was a success, and word spread around campus that the new professor was something special. By the end of the year, the Agriculture Department had seventy-six students. But George was still received coldly by faculty members who resented what they regarded as his professional arrogance

He studied hard, but he still had to take on odd jobs as a waiter, janitor, and laundryman to pay his way through school. He economized by sewing his own clothes and collecting discarded wrapping paper and pencil stubs for taking notes in class.

and his high salary, which, though it was much less than he had earned in Iowa, was much more than they earned. Being all light-skinned Negroes or mulattos, they also considered him inferior because his skin was dark and "too African-looking." At white colleges, George had been everyone's pet; now finally at a black college, it seems he was everyone's pet peeve. Even Washington seemed to be less than impressed with his new hire, who turned out to be jealous of his "turf," terrible at administrative duties, and often downright insubordinate. The two men would end up fighting for decades over differing academic priorities and leadership styles. But George was too busy to worry about any of these problems. He was administering an entire department, recruiting students, raising funds, lecturing at conferences, introducing new agricultural methods to local farmers, teaching classes, doing lab research, writing bulletins, serving on committees, and setting up an experiment station—all with far less equipment, staff, money, and support than was needed.[4]

He succeeded because he was like the Little Engine that Could in the beloved children's story of the same name. He was always telling himself, "I think I can, I think I can." He thought he could help rebuild the economy of the South, which had been devastated by the Civil War and "King Cotton." He thought he could free farmers from the sharecropping system—a form of servitude that was nearly as bad as the old plantation system because it left them in perpetual debt.[5] He thought he could overcome the suspicion, superstition, and ignorance that led many black and white Southerners to blame their troubles on northern

---

4   The entire budget for the Tuskegee Experiment Station, for example, was never more than $3,400, including staff salaries. Carver himself did not accept a raise for more than twenty years and as a result went from being the highest to the lowest paid teacher at the Institute.

5   Sharecroppers didn't own the land they worked. They were forced to rent it for the lion's share of their next crop and to buy seed and supplies on credit for exorbitant prices. At the turn of the century, 65 percent of all the farmers in Alabama were sharecroppers.

conspiracies by showing them how they could earn a good living and determine their own future. The wonderful thing was that George's confidence gradually grew like a mustard seed, first throughout the Tuskegee Institute and Macon County, then throughout Alabama and the South.

September 1916

Exhausted from laboring in the heat and humidity, the old black farmer bent to pick up his load of cotton, but it was too heavy. He sank to his knees and mopped his brow. Through the salty sweat that stung his rheumy eyes, he saw someone coming down the road. It was a stranger—a Negro stranger, so he relaxed. One had to be cautious these days.

"How do," he called out in a neighborly fashion.

"Good afternoon," the stranger returned in a soft, almost lyrical voice, "I'm Professor Carver." He was wearing a shabby old suit and floppy straw hat. He didn't look like a professor—at least that was what the farmer thought to himself. He had never actually met one before, but he was pretty certain they didn't dress like peddlers and drive rickety wagons loaded down with all sorts of parcels. "Mind if I rest a while? I've been on the road all day."

"Come on up to the house. I was just fixin' to sit a spell myself. I can't work in the fields like I used to. Time was when I could have lifted this hundred-pound bale like it was nothing a'tall. Now I cain't even lift one end."

George jumped down from the wagon and offered his services. He was no longer the frail and sickly child that had been rescued from Confederate raiders. Though he was in his early fifties now, he was tall, lanky, and strong. He lifted the bale and put it on the sledge. When he and the farmer reached the old, ramshackle cabin that lay at the edge of the field, a woman came out to greet them. She was not nearly as old as her husband, but she looked haggard and worn out. George took off his hat and thanked her kindly when she offered him a cup of water from the well. All three of them sat on the stoop, and he began to talk in his gentle yet convincing way.

"You know, I didn't grow up in these parts, but I have been studying the soil for twenty years, and I think that your farm would be perfect for planting peanuts."

"You mean goobers?" the farmer scoffed. "What good are they? There's no market for them. Besides, the only crop the landlord lets me plant is cotton."

"I know that's been true in the past," George admitted. "But times are changing. Over in Macon County, plenty of farmers are raising peanuts and sweet potatoes and selling them for a good profit, too. That's because there are all sorts of new ways to use them." He began unwrapping one of the bundles from his wagon. "Let me show you. I bet you never had coffee or griddle cakes made from peanuts, did you? Well, these samples are mighty delicious and easy to make, too."

George spent two hours with the old couple, and when he left, their faces were beaming. He had shown them a way to clear their most pressing debts and become self-sufficient, and he promised to return during the next planting season to see how they were getting on. He was late getting back to Tuskegee. He really shouldn't have stopped at their place or spent so much time with them, but the Peanut Man, as he was nicknamed, lived to make converts, and he didn't care if he made them one or two at a time. He said he was just following the example of the apostles.

Back at the Institute, he had a night class of thirty students waiting impatiently for him. He rushed into the *laboratory and apologized for his tardiness. Then he launched into his lecture with a question: "There are fourteen elements that plants feed upon and that keep the soil from wearing out. Who can name them all?"*

Eager hands shot up, but no one could name all fourteen, so George had to help them out by naming some himself. After two decades of teaching, he had learned to expect as much. Even students who had grown up on farms were woefully ignorant about such vital substances as nitrogen, carbon, hydrogen, iron, magnesium, phosphorus, and potassium.[6]

"Why must we memorize them all?" one young woman complained.

"Why?" echoed George. "We must because the Bible says, 'The earth is full of Thy riches.' If we are to mine the riches, we have to know what they are. When I first came to Alabama, I knew nothing about its flora and fauna. I had to ask someone every time I encountered a new plant, 'What do you call this?' I still have to ask about some, but I don't feel ignorant. I feel like Columbus sailing east across the Atlantic into uncharted waters. Just like him, I am discovering a new world, and it is incredibly exciting.

"You, the students in this class, are embarked on the same voyage of discovery. You are among the lucky few. Not many people have the opportunity to learn the things you will learn about Nature. So you have a tremendous responsibility to learn well, and then to share what you have learned with others in terms that they can understand. I met an old couple today who was still growing cotton on a tenant farm and hardly getting by, despite all their best efforts. Did I tell

---

6   George was among the first scientists to teach students about the Periodic Table (a list of "elements" or chemical substances that cannot be broken down), which was introduced in 1869.

*them that overdependence on this one crop was robbing the
soil of its nutrients? Did I lecture them on scientific farming
methods, or the economics of cutting production costs and
providing new goods for which there is a growing market
demand? No, of course I didn't. Instead, I gave them this
bulletin."* He waved a slim pamphlet in the air. "It's called
How to Grow the Peanut and 105 Ways of Preparing It for
Human Consumption. *It's written in simple English any lit-
erate person can understand. It has planting and cultivation
instructions as well as recipes for food preparation and stor-
age through the winter. The couple I met have agreed to try
it out, and I predict that within a few seasons they will be
planting acres and acres of peanuts.*

*"But you, ladies and gentlemen, are not farmers, at
least not yet. You are students, and you have come here to
learn the theory as well as the practice of agriculture. For
our next class, we are going to take a little field trip into
the woods, and I want you to look closely at all the plants
we encounter. You don't have to memorize their names, at
least not yet. I merely want you to admire their beauty and
become curious about their potential uses...."*

GEORGE SPOKE "in a plain conversational tone," which was as
unusual as it was welcome in an era of overblown rhetoric and
fancy oratory. He often "sprinkled his talks with subdued humor
and understated dramatic examples." He may have been trained as
a scientist, but he taught science as if it were a fascinating detective
story full of twists and turns. He also thought of it as a perfect
expression of the three ideal stages in human development:
"Finding, Adapting, and Creating." One of his pupils, who went
on to become a distinguished professor of agriculture in his own
right, declared that George was always "guiding students to discover things for themselves rather than telling them everything."

When he was a six-year-old, the future vice president of the United States, Henry Wallace, used to tag along with George on his morning rambles through the countryside. He described George as "the kindliest, most patient teacher I ever knew....He could cause a little boy to see things which he saw in a grass flower." George's style was compelling and charismatic. But even more important, it reflected his missionary zeal for reaching "the man farthest down," even if he was just a struggling first-year student.[7]

When he arrived at Tuskegee, he found that his students were hardly the cream of the crop. Most had only a grade school education, and some were practically illiterate. Lecturing on abstract concepts was definitely out of the question. So, he would choose one simple organism like the cow pea plant and ask them to study it in depth. In this way, they learned the basics not only of chemistry, biochemistry, and botany but also such related subjects as meteorology and entomology. He created a special museum filled with specimens of animals, minerals, and plants for students to see and touch. He arranged for them to compete against one another and perform their own laboratory experiments. He took them on field expeditions. He dared them to stump him by bringing items to identify. One enterprising group decided to play a trick on him by gluing together the head of an ant, the body of a beetle, and the legs of a spider. Peering at it through his old microscope, George confirmed that it was indeed a new kind of insect—a humbug!

He also freely shared his "demonstration approach" with other teachers through conferences and pamphlets. He wrote that "every teacher should realize that a very large proportion of every true student's work must be outside the classroom." He went on to add that all children should have gardens, for "even if the child does not become an agriculturist or a farmer, these things all have

---

7   *The Man Farthest Down* was the title of a popular book by Booker T. Washington. He and George used the phrase often, and it revealed their mutual dedication to helping the least fortunate members of society climb the ladder of success.

a tendency to make the child think, and that is what we are trying to teach him—to think." George's door was always open, even to students in other departments. A grateful young undergraduate once remarked, "When advice is sought by the humblest student, there is no 'red tape' to encounter in entering his office." At the students' request, he also taught a Sunday evening Bible class. Over a hundred students attended regularly. Some of his favorite maxims delivered in this forum were: "Be wise as a serpent and harmless as a dove," and, "Do not look up to the rich or down to the poor."

He and Washington were also instrumental in establishing fifty black elementary and secondary schools throughout Macon County. Such institutions were welcomed like rain after a long dry season. Blacks remembered all too well when it was forbidden to learn how to read and write, and thus they prized learning.[8] For adults, George organized monthly Farmers Institutes and an annual Farmers Conference that drew hundreds of participants. And there was the Tuskegee Experiment Station's traveling "school." Modeled after the Seed Corn Gospel Trains started by other experiment stations, it was simply a wagon (and later, an automobile) equipped with sample seeds, farm products, and demonstration materials, but it had an enormous impact since it allowed George and his students to reach, on average, two thousand people a year.

George was indeed the South's most popular and effective preacher of the new gospel of soil conservation. He infected his audiences "with the same childlike awe he felt for the miracles of nature." One white listener described his magnetic quality: "The most striking thing about him is his eyes, which are deep black but which seem to have two gleaming coals of living fire behind them.

---

8   In the early twentieth century, there were as many as ten million blacks in the South but only a few hundred black schools and only twenty-five black colleges. These were small and poorly funded. Reportedly most black teachers were paid less than it cost to hire convict labor. Nonetheless, black literacy jumped from 3 percent in 1865 to 70 percent in 1910.

His skin is extremely dark, but when he begins to talk, race and color are lost sight of and one hears a wonderfully soft, musical voice telling a story of God's bounty and of man's indifference to the great gifts spread before him on every hand." Another observer says he taught people that the "great creative forces of the universe were divine in origin, and the man who attuned himself to these forces could harness their power and become an agent for the creation of the miraculous." On a practical level, George's preaching was rewarded by measurable economic progress among southern blacks. As Washington reported in his 1911 book, *My Larger Education*, "By encouraging Negro farmers to buy land and improve their methods of agriculture, it has multiplied the number of small landowners and increased the tax value of the land. Recent investigations show that the number of Negro landowners in Macon County has grown more in the last five or six years than in the whole previous period since the abolition of slavery. Land that was selling for two to three dollars an acre five years ago is now worth fifteen and twenty dollars an acre."

George was "the kindliest, most patient teacher I ever knew....He could cause a little boy to see things which he saw in a grass flower."

George himself said that his efforts were directed toward encouraging people to regard Nature as the greatest teacher of all. He passionately believed that Nature produces no waste and that man has only to apply his intelligence to discover uses for supposedly useless resources. On the Tuskegee Institute Experiment Station, he tested his beliefs. Because poor farmers couldn't afford to spend much, he concentrated on using the most basic materials and methods. For instance, since he knew that commercial fertilizer was expensive, he tried enriching the soil with cow peas, velvet beans, and corn—plants that actually put nitrogen back into the ground instead of using it up. When he began his "green manuring" experiment, a one-acre plot yielded a net loss of $2.40, but within a few years the same plot produced a net profit of

$94.65. He published the results in *How to Build Up Worn Out Soils,* stating he was "keeping in mind the poor tenant farmer with a one-horse equipment." But this was just the beginning. George spent decades experimenting with "hybridization," i.e., cross-breeding plants to come up with new varieties that would produce bigger and better results. The challenge was great, for when he started out, genetics was a new and almost unknown field.[9]

In another pioneering experiment, he used leaves, mulch, and food waste as organic fertilizer. He thought of this method after he found enormous pumpkin vines measuring almost forty feet in length growing out of the rubbish pile at the institute. He argued that using compost was "the cheapest and most effective way of reclaiming barren land." But his was a lone voice; all the other agricultural experts of the day claimed that a new miracle product—synthetic fertilizer—was the answer to the South's soil exhaustion. They failed to realize, as he did, that poor farmers couldn't afford a miracle that cost seventeen cents a pound.

George was also years ahead of other agriculturists with bulletins like *Experiments with Sweet Potatoes* and *Successful Yields of Small Grains.* Such bi-annual publications were distributed at no charge to 2,500 farmers all over the South. They asked "every farmer to send samples of soils, grains, fertilizers, fodder, grasses, insects, feeding stuffs, etc." for analysis, and invited "every farmer within reach, to visit our station frequently and come in more direct touch with us." In terms of content, they covered everything from basic farming instructions and crop rotation schedules to organic treatments for plant diseases and insect control. While the bulletins published by other stations were highly technical, Tuskegee's written in laymen's terms and they included such mundane material as household hints, recipes, and herbal remedies. This was because they weren't meant to impress scientists; they

---

9   In 1900, records of the dwarf pea experiments conducted by a nineteenth-century Austrian monk and botanist, Gregor Mendel, were unearthed, and genetics—the study of inherited characteristics—finally gained credibility.

were directed at farmers and farm wives who were set in their ways and often pathologically suspicious of change. To convince them to try his new agricultural methods, George had to give them practical incentives that they could immediately understand and appreciate. So he made it his life's work to discover hundreds of ways for them to use "good-for-nothing" crops, plants, and natural resources to make valuable commercial products and to become healthy and self-sufficient. Here is a brief rundown of some of his accomplishments in this regard:

- He taught farmers to stop the ruinous practice of burning fields after the harvest season and to turn the soil over so the crop waste could act as a natural fertilizer. (He likened burning to setting a match to the outside bills on a roll of greenbacks.)

- His experiments with sweet potatoes defied the belief of many experts. Fields that had typically produced only 37 bushels began to yield 266 bushels an acre.

- He convinced farmers who frowned on wasting acreage and effort on truck gardens for personal consumption that vegetables could be an important addition to their vitamin-deficient diet, which was usually restricted to pork fat, cornmeal, hominy, and molasses. Indeed, he was one of the rare few outside the medical community who understood that malnutrition was a major factor in susceptibility to disease.

- He conducted a major survey for the U.S. Department of Agriculture on medicinal plants.

- As a self-professed "cookstove chemist," he popularized new methods of curing and pickling and new preventions against the spread of germs and bacteria. He also favored dehydration of fruits and vegetables since farmers could seldom afford to buy jars, cans, or preservatives like sugar.

➤ During World War I, he devised ways of feeding the troops overseas and, on the domestic front, he helped industry replace German supplies of wheat flour with sweet potato flour and commercial dyes with home-grown vegetable dyes.

➤ He convinced farmers to substitute corn and acorns for expensive commercial livestock feed, noting that "the great quantity of acorns produced in our oak forests... have been heretofore practically a waste product."

➤ He introduced thirteen new varieties of cotton, some of which not only produced a third more bolls but also matured early, before boll weevils could destroy them.[10]

➤ Knowing that the large part of most crops is composed of inedible waste, he made a variety of useful household products—from rugs and paints to cold remedies and synthetic marble—from soybeans, okra, dandelion, black oak, sweet gum, willow, swamp maple, chicken feathers, wood ashes, saw-dust, and pine needles.

➤ He experimented with commercially viable alternatives to cotton, like rice, sugarcane, and sugar beets, and could produce an amazing three tons of alfalfa per acre through organic fertilization.

---

10 First found in the U.S. in 1904, this devastating pest—a beetle that lays its eggs in the heart of the cotton plant and feeds off its bolls and blossoms—infested 51,300 square miles of Alabama by 1921.

→ He used native clays to make whitewash and brilliantly colored dyes. Some of his stains were one-tenth the cost of commercial varieties. From clay, he also manufactured talcum and face powders, a laundry bluing agent, a metal polish, and a bedbug repellent.

→ He helped a colleague identify the fungi of Alabama, personally contributing sixty-four specimens. He also sent eight hundred botanical specimens to the U.S. Department of Agriculture. The department's experts were stunned to learn that, armed only with an old microscope, he had identified all but one accurately and discovered several new species.

Before long everyone in Macon County knew George as the "Peanut Man." He had become the father of a whole new industry.

Of course, not all of George's experiments worked, and not all of the products he created were marketed commercially. He planted a mulberry grove at the Tuskegee station in order to raise valuable silkworms that fed on the leaves, but he couldn't get farmers interested in silk production. Passersby were awestruck by the station's superior cotton fields, but no one, outside of some farmers in Australia and Africa, tried his new hybrids. He also failed dismally at poultry raising, sheep raising, and beekeeping. As he often liked to observe, however, his failures taught him as much as his successes. What were research and experimentation all about except trial and error? That was part of the excitement. One never knew where the next experiment might lead. When asked how he planned to develop this or that discovery for profit, he would inevitably reply, "I have done all I intend to. My interest is scientific and not financial. If an investigator goes into business, he ceases to be an investigator and becomes a businessman....It is for the people to take these products and create supply and demand."

IN 1903, HE TESTED PEANUTS—a relatively recent import from South America—for the first time. Peanuts are a fruit (not a nut, despite the name) that is easy to cultivate and that naturally enriches the soil in which it is grown. Pound for pound, George realized peanuts had more protein than steak and more carbohydrates than potatoes. To prove peanuts' versatility, he had the senior girls at Tuskegee use them to prepare an entire meal for Principal Washington and a special delegation of visitors. The menu included soup, mock chicken, salad, bread, candy, cookies, ice cream, and coffee. Then he published his famous bulletin on peanuts, which included directions for making butter, cheese, buttermilk, Worcester sauce, chili sauce, flour, breakfast food, ink, wood filler, packing material, detergent, salves, bleach, shaving cream, shampoo, plastic, linoleum, axle grease, and synthetic rubber.[11] Before long, as mentioned, everyone in Macon County knew George as the "Peanut Man." He had become the father of a whole new industry. Farmers who thought they would never be able to plant anything but cotton gradually discovered that the "goober" was a highly marketable product. It not only cost very little to plant but it was resistant to disease, drought, and the dreaded boll weevil, which had become the scourge of the South. The first commercial crops were grown in 1917; by the 1940s, peanuts were the second most important cash crop in the South, accounting for $200 million in sales and covering five million acres. Macon County, home of the Tuskegee Institute, saw the most dramatic improvement. In 1915, the county was on the verge of bankruptcy; by 1919, thanks to George's discoveries, it was the most prosperous county in the state. Today, peanuts are still one of the South's most important crops, providing roasted and raw snacks, peanut butter, cooking oil, margarine, soap, and dozens of other products.

---

11 Peanut milk was one product that actually saved countless lives in regions in Africa, where it was not possible to raise cows and where malnutrition and disease meant that mothers often were unable to nurse their infant children.

By 1916, George had earned an international scientific reputation, even though he didn't possess a Ph.D. This was the year he was nominated as a board member of the prestigious National Agricultural Society and as a fellow of the even more exclusive Royal Society for the Arts in Great Britain. As an indefatigable champion of black economic independence, he was also widely acknowledged as an important leader in the civil rights movement. His message was that discrimination and poverty were obstacles that could be largely overcome by hard work and persistence, but he was no Pollyanna. He was well aware that the Civil War and Reconstruction had left behind a legacy of hatred and violence. Most emancipated blacks were unprepared for freedom. They had no food, no clothes, no homes, no skills, and no jobs. They had been accustomed to a system in which submission and apathy equaled survival. White landlords still routinely whipped black tenants and treated them as chattel. Secret societies devoted to white supremacy were organized to spread fear and intimidation. Laws protecting the rights of black citizens were seldom enforced. In 1896, the Supreme Court legalized segregation in *Plessy* v. *Ferguson*, a case that perverted the equal protection clause of the Fourteenth Amendment in order to condone "separate but equal" facilities for whites and blacks. During World War I, segregation of the troops led to sometimes brutal treatment of black soldiers. Worst of all, the murderous practice of lynching continued unabated. During the "Red Summer" of 1919, for example, seventy blacks were killed, and there were twenty-five major race riots.

Racism was real and it was dangerous, George admitted, but he was adamant that it should not be an excuse for failure or for permanent victimhood.

George himself had direct experience with racism. When he was young, he had worked for at least one white employer, the wife of a prosperous ranch owner in Kansas, who believed "the colored were born to be servants" and who subjected him to nearly every kind of indignity. All his adult life, he had known that he must step off the sidewalk and stand in the gutter when whites passed. He must take his hat off when he spoke to them and say "Yes, sir" and "No, sir."[12] He was never to speak to white ladies in public or ride on the same seat with them in a carriage or, later, in an automobile. And he could never claim the right to be called "Mister" or even "Carver"; blacks were always called by their first names as when they were slaves. When he traveled around the country, he felt the full weight of Jim Crow laws. There were no sleeping cars for blacks on trains, no accommodations at hotels, and no tables at restaurants. Even when he lectured at colleges or at professional conferences as an honored guest, he was not invited to dine with his hosts. On one occasion, he was refused entrance to a hotel where he was to deliver the keynote address at a special event. He had to be smuggled in via the freight elevator. At a black school he was visiting in Mississippi, a white mob chased him into the fields and shot at him. And when Vice President Coolidge came to the Tuskegee Institute shortly after World War I to dedicate a hospital for black veterans, the Ku Klux Klan in Atlanta assembled a small army to launch a midnight attack—an army that rapidly retreated when it realized that it was facing a gauntlet of several hundred students and battle-hardened veterans standing shoulder to shoulder in the dark.

Racism was real and it was dangerous, George admitted, but he was adamant that it should not be an excuse for failure or for permanent victimhood. He urged blacks not to waste time on bitterness or resentment. And he showed them how to help themselves and become self-reliant by teaching them to do "common things in an uncommon way." In 1908, he wrote:

In these strenuous times, we are likely to become morbid and look constantly upon the dark side of life, and spend entirely too much

---

12 This was no small precaution. One of the other teachers at the Tuskegee Institute failed to say "Yes, sir" to a local store proprietor and was knifed.

time considering and brooding over what we can't do, rather than what we can do, and instead of growing morose and despondent over opportunities, either real or imaginary that are shut from us, let us rejoice at the many explored fields in which there is unlimited fame and fortune to the successful explorer and upon which there is no color line....

He also wrote that "hate for our fellow man puts us in a living hell," and he exhorted:

Fear of something is the root of hate for others, and hate within will eventually destroy the hater. Keep your thoughts free from hate, and you will have no fear from those who hate you. David, though small, was filled with truth, right thinking, and good will for others. Goliath represents one who let fear into his heart, and it stayed there long enough to grow into hate for others.

For those who remained unmoved by a spiritual argument, he offered a practical one based on his observations about economics and farming in the Deep South, where lack of native industry was, in his opinion, a problem that must be solved before racism could be addressed:

The virgin fertility of our soils and the vast amount of unskilled labor have been a curse rather than a blessing to agriculture. This exhaustive system for cultivation, the destruction of forests, the rapid and almost constant decomposition of organic matter...make our agricultural problem one requiring more brains than that of the North, East, or West. By the advance of civilization, the markets have become more fastidious; and he who puts such a product on the market as it demands, controls the market, regardless of color.

As a civil rights leader who was neither a militant nor an "Uncle Tom," and as a gentle, soft-spoken, and kind person who treated everyone he met the same, whether they were white or black, rich or poor, George won public praise from such diametrically opposed groups as the Daughters of the Confederacy and the National Association for the Advancement of Colored Peoples. He made friends in all camps because he was realistic and tolerant. He knew that it takes time to win people over; he had been winning them over his entire life by practicing simple, every-day virtues.

In his letter of acceptance to the Tuskegee Institute, George declared, "It has always been the one ideal of my life to be of the greatest good to the greatest number of 'my people' possible and to this end I have been preparing myself for these many years; feeling as I do that this line of education is the key to unlock the golden door of freedom...." It was an ideal that he continued to try to live up to for almost half a century. Despite his initial reluctance, he remained at Tuskegee for forty-seven years. He turned down many tempting offers to pursue a brilliant and rewarding career elsewhere.[13]

IN 1939, HIS HEALTH began to fail. He suffered from pernicious anemia and chronic bouts of influenza. Vitamin injections helped, but only temporarily. Nonetheless, George's last years were among his busiest and most productive. He became a philanthropist, giving money and help, often anonymously, to the poor. He organized and helped underwrite a foundation and museum to preserve his work at the institute. He traveled and lectured widely. He delivered broadcasts on the radio, and he was the subject of numerous newspaper stories. He counted among his friends such important figures as Henry Ford and Andrew Carnegie and every president from William McKinley to Franklin D. Roosevelt. He received fan mail from around the world. Although he could not

---

[13] George contemplated marrying a young woman he courted after arriving at Tuskegee, but she did not share his interests in the botanical world, and so he decided to dedicate himself to teaching and research.

answer it all (he was receiving over 150 letters a day at the peak of his fame), he did keep up a voluminous correspondence. He especially liked to respond to letters from alumni who had gone on to found "little Tuskegees" throughout the South.[14] Then, on January 5, 1943, the man who had been a sickly slave child and who was not expected to live through infancy, finally died at age seventy-nine. He was buried alongside Booker T. Washington on the campus they both loved so much. His adoptive mother, Susan Carver, would have been most pleased to know that her prophesy had been fulfilled. George Washington Carver had become someone "mighty special," indeed. He had become a living symbol of the divine spark of creativity that lies within all of us.

SUGGESTED READINGS

I relied on two fine although very different biographies for most of the factual information in this chapter: Linda O. McMurry's *George Washington Carver: Scientist and Symbol* (New York: Oxford University Press, 1981) and Rackham Holt's *George Washington Carver: A Biography* (Garden City, NY: Doubleday, Doran & Co., 1943). There are also two fictional accounts of George's life that make for worthwhile reading: Shirley Graham and George D. Lipscomb, *Dr. George Washington Carver: A Scientist* (New York, Julian Messner, 1944); and Anne Terry White, *George Washington Carver: The Story of a Great American* (New York: Random House, 1953).

---

[14] Today, the Tuskegee Institute is home to the Carver Foundation and the Tuskegee Agricultural Research and Experiment Station, both of which are dedicated to the natural sciences. It also features schools of arts and sciences, engineering, nursing, and education for over 3,000 students.

Robert E. Lee

Gallant Soldier

(1807–1870)

The man who could still smile, who was selfless in his compassion for others, the old gray warrior in the armor of a shining heart.

—Earl Schenck Meirs
Robert E. Lee

It is well that war is so terrible, [lest] we should grow too fond of it!

—Robert E. Lee
Witnessing an enemy charge
repulsed at Fredericksburg
December 1862

June 1837

    Almost as long as memory recorded—since the days when ancient Indian tribes wandered the land—the Mississippi River had been called the "Father of the Waters." The third longest river system in the world, rivaled only by the Nile and the Amazon, it began in northwestern Minnesota and flowed more than two thousand miles to Louisiana where it emptied millions of gallons of water into the Gulf of Mexico.

    The tall and handsome young lieutenant with erect military bearing, wavy black hair, and deep brown eyes leaned over the rail of the steamboat, contemplated this terrible adversary, and sighed. He had a formidable job ahead of him, and he wasn't at all sure that he was up to it. In fact, the U.S. Corps of Engineers had actually charged him with three Herculean tasks. First, he was to eliminate all obstacles to navigation in a fifteen-mile series of rapids in Illinois. Second, he was to tame an even more treacherous eleven-mile stretch in Iowa. Third—and he could hardly believe it—he was to divert the entire course of the Mississippi. The reason? It seemed that years of erosion and shifting sand and silt had caused the mighty waters to turn away from St. Louis, and this threatened to put Missouri's most important port out of business.

    Well, there was no point in dwelling on the difficulty of these tasks, or on the fact that he had almost no men or funds at his disposal, or on the problem that was troubling him most of all—being lonesome and homesick, separated as he was from his beloved children. It was high time to roll up his sleeves and get to work. So, Robert left the railing and returned to his tiny, cramped cabin which was strewn with maps and diagrams. It was here, on paper, that he would plan his campaign. Then he would fight one battle at a time until he had achieved all his objectives.

ROBERT EDWARD LEE was literally "to the manor born" on January 19, 1807, at the Stratford Manor plantation in Stratford, Virginia. He was the son of the great Revolutionary War hero, Light Horse Harry Lee. Harry was a daring, brilliant, and flamboyant cavalry officer, a member of the Continental Congress, a governor of Virginia, and a Federalist congressman in the U.S. House of Representatives. He was also a reckless and profligate gambler who squandered his wife's fortune, who was once imprisoned for debt, who flirted with treason by conspiring against his mentor, George Washington, and who deserted his family when his actions caught up with him. From a self-imposed exile in the Caribbean, he was wont to write eloquent letters full of learned observations and sound moral advice (that he himself never followed) for his elder sons. But he never once wrote to Robert; in fact, only once in a passing reference did he even acknowledge his existence.

This mixed legacy, bequeathed by a man he barely knew, shaped Robert's own character.[1] He cherished a romantic ideal of his father's bravery and military genius, but he also faced the hard reality: Harry was dissipated, irresponsible, and concerned only with satisfying his own selfish desires. If you could sum up in a single word what Harry's character lacked and what Robert's character possessed in abundance, the word would be *loyalty*. Throughout his life, Robert sacrificed everything in order to fulfill his deep sense of loyalty and obligation to his family, his friends, his comrades-in-arms, and his home, which was the sovereign state of Virginia.

Robert's mother, Ann Carter Lee, provided a real-life model of loyalty in action. She never repudiated her husband and remained true to him no matter how much he disappointed or disgraced her. She turned a blind eye to his indiscretions. She sold all the manor's

---

1   Harry abandoned the family when Robert was six and died when he was eleven.

furniture and moved the family into a few bare downstairs rooms so she could honor his mounting debts. When his eldest child by a previous marriage came of age in 1810, Ann Lee vacated the manor so that he could have sole possession. From then on, she and her children lived a vagabond life. Never again would they have a permanent refuge. Robert, the fifth of Harry and Ann's six children, knew full well how difficult it was for his mother to keep what was left of the family together, especially since she was suffering more and more from an undiagnosed complaint that was most likely tuberculosis.

She did scrape up enough funds to send young Robert to boarding school. He was shy and withdrawn, but he excelled at mathematics. At age thirteen, with one brother away at Harvard and another in the navy, he came back to Alexandria where his mother and sisters were living. As the male head of the household, he not only kept up with his studies but also did the marketing, supervised the household servants, nursed his mother, and cared for his sisters. "Old beyond his years," he took on adult responsibilities with a cheerful and contented demeanor. After a year of trying, he finally managed at eighteen to secure an appointment to the U.S. Military Academy at West Point along the Hudson River in New York. Why did he choose West Point? His education would be free, and he would learn two valuable trades: soldiering and engineering. He wanted more than anything else to support his mother and sisters, and West Point offered the best opportunity. But perhaps some small part of Robert also wanted to follow in the footsteps of his father.

It was a hard life at West Point. Cadets could leave the post only once for two weeks in four years. Over half of all those who entered dropped out, unable to endure the miserable food, the uncomfortable barracks, the heavy classload, the grueling marches, and the endless infantry drills. Robert not only survived but flourished in this demanding environment. He worked diligently to earn high marks in mathematics, chemistry, physics, geography, history, law, ethics, French, drawing, and military engineering. He particularly enjoyed the last, which emphasized "field fortification, permanent fortification, artillery, grand tactics, and civil and military architecture." While still a cadet, he was offered an acting assistant professorship in mathematics, which meant tutoring other cadets for $10 a month on top of his $16 pay and $12 subsistence allowance. Virtually all of this went for room, board, uniforms, and other essentials. He was extremely frugal and rarely spent any money on personal items.

In 1829, at age twenty-two, he graduated second in his class without incurring a single demerit in four years—a rare and perhaps unique feat that reveals the depths of his integrity and self-discipline; typically, cadets racked up dozens or even hundreds of demerits. He was then granted a commission as a second lieutenant in the U.S. Corps of Engineers and a few months' leave. He returned to Virginia in June to find his ailing mother on her deathbed. She lasted barely a month.

Robert sacrificed everything in order to fulfill his deep sense of loyalty to his family, his friends, his comrades-in-arms, and his home.

Robert was suddenly bereft of family. His father and mother were dead. His brothers and sisters were grown and living apart. He had no home but the army, and since he had yet to receive his first assignment, he didn't have the slightest idea where "home" would end up being. It was an unsettling experience. One of his few consolations while he bided his time and waited for orders was his visits to an old childhood friend, Mary Custis, the great-granddaughter of George and Martha Washington. At the end of his leave, when he was ordered to report to Cockspur Island at Savannah, Georgia, he secured leave from Mary's father to write to her.

And he wrote regularly, even though the job in Georgia took up virtually all his daylight hours. He and a handful of officers were charged with building a fort on a tiny spit of land that was mostly marsh and swamp. They worked side by side with hired laborers, "armpit deep in mud and water," creating ditches and dikes and laying foundations. On a long leave in 1830, Robert proposed to Mary. Her father denied consent, but the couple considered themselves engaged. When Robert returned to Georgia, he found that most of the previous season's work had been destroyed by storms. It was an ill omen—the fort would not be completed for nearly twenty years. In early 1831, however, he was reassigned to a less arduous fort-building project at Old Point, Virginia. And in June he finally received permission to wed Mary. The couple moved to a new station, Fort Monroe, and lived there in humble rented lodgings until 1834. Mary came from a prosperous plantation family and was used to having every whim indulged. She hated army life and found excuses—usually some form of hypochondria—to go home to her parents for months at a time. Once more ensconced in the lap of luxury, she began a lifelong habit of writing carping letters to her husband, who, in her opinion, was always wanting for one reason or another.

Robert was deeply disappointed, but he was also relieved to be left alone to pursue his career. After a short time, it had become painfully clear that he and his wife displayed quite different dispositions. But, like his mother Ann, he resolved to remain faithful—a vow he would keep for four decades. And there was another bond that united him to Mary—the birth of seven children: Custis in 1832, Mary in 1835, Rooney in 1837, Annie in 1839, Agnes in 1841, Rob in 1843, and Mildred in 1846. Robert was devoted to each. In contrast to the prevailing attitude of the day, he believed children "should be governed by *love,* not *fear.*" He was playful and affectionate when many of his contemporaries were stern and authoritarian. He also took a deep and abiding interest in his sons' and daughters' education and character development.[2]

In 1834, Robert was transferred to Washington, D.C., as an assistant to the chief of the Engineer Corps. His new job required

---

2   Once again, he was exorcising the ghost of Harry Lee, the father who had cared so little about him.

him to learn about the vast bureaucracy that was starting to emerge in the army. He also gained valuable experience on a surveying expedition to the Great Lakes region. In 1836, he was promoted to first lieutenant and in 1837 was transferred again, this time to Missouri. Thirty years old and full of restless ambition, he was pleased and excited, but then, he had yet to see his "assignment." As the beginning of this chapter notes, he had to render two long stretches of rapids permanently navigable and divert the course of the Mississippi River back toward St. Louis.

He spent a great deal of time consulting existing maps and drawing engineering diagrams. But he quickly learned that these count for little unless one has actually seen a problem firsthand and studied it. In one instance, he changed his mind about his whole approach for clearing the rapids. The most common practice was to utilize steam-driven "snagboats" specially designed to remove timber, brush, and submerged rock. But the rapids in this case were constantly filling up with new obstacles, and during the dry season they were too shallow for easy passage. After making his own more accurate maps and taking countless soundings, Robert determined that completely new channels would have to be created by blasting and dredging. But when he examined the river as it neared St. Louis, he concluded that dredging and blasting were not the answer. These methods were too expensive and time-consuming, and they had already been tried without success. An elaborate system of dams and dikes would have to be built instead. He advised the city fathers to "work with, not against, the river," and he explained how his plan would actually allow the Mississippi to do the heavy work; the dams and dikes would encourage it to wash away the massive sandbar that blocked the harbor and that had so far resisted all attempts at dredging.

Robert was not an advocate of slavery. He wrote in 1856, "In this enlightened age, there are few, I believe, but what will acknowledge that slavery as an institution is a moral & political evil in any Country."

After an intense lobbying effort, he convinced them to join Congress in supplying the necessary start-up capital. In 1837, he felt confident enough to return home to Virginia to fetch his family. At this point, he was happier, perhaps, than ever before. He was testing his engineering skills on a grand scale, and he was raising his brood. In 1838, he was promoted to the rank of captain. "Promotion in peacetime was rare," a biographer pointed out, and Robert's rapid advancement revealed his strength as a leader. But not everything was going well. There were the long construction delays because of the weather and the difficulties of working on a shoestring budget. Before long, Mary insisted on taking the children back to Virginia. In 1840, the funds needed to complete the project petered out. Robert was ordered to return to Washington. It must have a bitter experience to have invested so much time and effort only to have to call it quits. (Later, other engineers would successfully finish the great project Robert had started, but he must have finished it in his dreams many times over.) His next assignment was in Brooklyn, New York. For six years, he worked hard to rebuild four military installations that had fallen into disrepair. Then, in 1846, he was called to war for the first time. He had used his training and experience to become one of the best engineers in the country, but what kind of warrior was he? Was he truly the heir of Light Horse Harry? This would be the test.

The Mexican War (1846–1848) was precipitated by the annexation of Texas, which became the twenty-eighth state in 1845. Mexico refused to recognize the state's Rio Grande border and broke off diplomatic relations. U.S. President James K. Polk, an ardent expansionist, sent troops to the disputed territory in the spring of 1846, and when Mexico responded with force, he declared war against the alleged invaders. Robert privately thought Polk had erred, but he applied for active duty and waited impatiently until his orders came through in August. He wrote his will—the only one he ever made—and set off for San Antonio where he would join a seven-hundred-mile expedition into the heart of Mexico.

It was a journey of discovery in literal and metaphorical terms. "For the first time in American history, United States armies marched on foreign soil and fought battles in an alien land." Detailed maps and reliable guides were impossible to come by. Scouting ahead in enemy territory at great risk, Robert was one of the intrepid few who became the eyes and ears of the army. On one occasion, he dived for cover under a log by a spring just as a large group of Mexican soldiers arrived to fill their canteens. He froze, thinking they would move on in a minute and he would be safe. But they sat down for a long rest—on the very log under which he was hidden. Worse yet, they were only the first in an unending procession of soldiers—an entire army was on the march! He remained motionless and silent for hours. Only after dark was he able to crawl out and head back to camp.

After many months, he still had not fired his weapon or stood on the battlefield, and this galled him. Then, in 1847, at the age of forty, he rode into combat during General Winfield Scott's assault on Mexico City. His first experience under fire came one night when he and another scout were returning from a reconnaissance mission. They were fired upon point-blank by one of their own sentries who stood no more than a dozen feet away. A rifle ball passed between Robert's arm and his side, singeing his uniform. He was more frustrated than scared, but he had no time to define his emotions. Scott ordered him to set up artillery batteries. He did so, directing fire in several important engagements and going for days on end without sleep. He also went on more dangerous reconnaissances, discovering routes to the capital and other key cities through supposedly impassable mountains. These routes were hailed as "making the difference between victory and defeat."

He had survived battle and had done so with a valor that would earn him three brevets (honorary field promotions). Meanwhile, the horror and injustice of war was not lost on him. He wrote to his family of the Mexican villagers caught in the crossfire: "My heart bled for the inhabitants...it was terrible to think of the women and children....You have no idea what a horrible sight a battlefield is." One day, in the midst of fierce fighting, he encountered a young peasant girl trying to help a wounded boy trapped beneath the body of a dying Mexican soldier. He ordered his men to free the boy and take him and the soldier to the U.S. field hospital for immediate treatment. Then he wheeled his horse and returned to the fray. He was also sympathetic to the fate of his own fellows: "No one at their comfortable homes can realize the exertions, pains & hardships of an Army in the field...." He stopped short of describing men killed with bayonets and blown to bits by mortar shells, but his letters convey terrible images nonetheless.

The war ended when Mexico City fell in September of 1847. In the treaty signed the following year, the United States gained vast lands—the future states of Arizona, California, Colorado, Nevada, New Mexico, and Utah. It also gained a new problem, one that was so fraught with controversy that it would eventually lead to another war. The problem, of course, was what to do about slavery in the west. The Compromise of 1850 guaranteed that California would be admitted as a free state, but the residents of other territories could determine whether they would apply for admission as slave or free states. Robert was ambivalent about the issue. On the one hand, he had grown up in a world in which slavery was unquestioned. His family and his wife's family owned slaves. He inherited a number of them, and when they ran away, he posted rewards for their return. Modern African Americans who despise the "cult worship" of Robert E. Lee in the Old South are perfectly correct when they point out that this was a man "who pledged his life to the defense of the social order that held their forefathers in bondage." But looking at the whole man and all his attitudes gives us a far more complex and far more sympathetic picture. Robert was not an advocate of slavery. He wrote in 1856, "In this enlightened age, there are few, I believe, but what will acknowledge that slavery as an institution is a moral & political evil in any Country." His own experience as a slaveholder had "soured" him on the practice. He clearly wished to see slavery abolished, but he thought immediate abolition would be a disaster. Where would the freedmen live? How would they earn their living? In the 1850s, he joined an organization that helped slaves purchase their freedom and return to Africa. He even paid the passage for those of his slaves who wished to go. Yet he knew that this was only a first step and, like Abraham Lincoln, he preached patience:

> ...emancipation will sooner result from the mild and mellowing influence of Christianity, than the storms and tempests of fiery Controversy. This influence, though slow, is sure.
>
> The doctrines and miracles of our Savior have required nearly two thousand years, to Convert but a small part of the human race, and even among Christian nations, what gross errors still exist!...
>
> While we see the Course of the final abolition of human Slavery is onward, and we give it the aid of our prayers and all justifiable means in our power, we must leave the progress as well as the result in his hands who sees the end, who Chooses to work by slow influence; and with whom two thousand years are but as a Single day.

He also predicted that any attempt to force the South to abandon slavery immediately would only lead to violence. Tragically, in 1861, his prediction would come true. But in the intervening years, Robert had too much on his mind to worry about another war. As soon as he was released from active duty in Mexico, he was sent to Baltimore, Maryland, to work on coastal defenses. The pile driver and the crane rather than the cannon and the musket were once more his weapons, and the battle was waged against the elements—wind, sand, and surf that continually assaulted the forts along the Atlantic coast. He spent much of the year 1849 sick with malaria, which he had contracted south of the border.

IN 1852, HE WAS APPOINTED superintendent of West Point. He hated the idea of being tied to a desk as a teacher and an administrator, but orders were orders. He held the post until 1855 when he became a lieutenant colonel in the Second Cavalry. A year later, he went to West Texas to oversee the Commanche reservation. He requested a long leave in 1857. His father-in-law had died and left the family saddled with debts and all their business affairs in sad confusion. While attempting to sort things out in Virginia, he was ordered to lead a company of marines that captured John Brown, a fanatical abolitionist who had seized the federal arsenal and was holding hostages at Harpers Ferry in 1859. Even though things appeared to settle down after Brown's execution, he feared there was worse to come. Back in Texas in January 1861, a month after South Carolina became the first state to secede, he wrote to Mary, "As far as I can judge from the papers we are between a state of anarchy & civil war."

On February 1, Texas seceded "and for the second time in twenty-five years proclaimed itself an independent republic." On February 9, delegates from Texas, South Carolina, Mississippi, Alabama, Georgia, Louisiana, and Florida formed the provisional government of the Confederate States of America.[3] Robert was recalled to Washington immediately by his old commander, Winfield Scott. Upon his departure from Texas, he confided to a friend, "If Virginia stands by the old Union, so will I. But if she secedes (though I do not believe in secession as a constitutional right, nor that there is sufficient cause for revolution), then I will follow my native State with my sword, and, if need be, with my life." In the meantime, however,

---

3   Virginia, Tennessee, Arkansas, and North Carolina joined the Confederacy after the attack on Fort Sumter.

he accepted a promotion to full colonel and command of the First Cavalry regiment. On March 4, Abraham Lincoln assumed office. About this time, Robert was offered a commission as a brigadier general in the Confederate army. He refused. On April 17 (five days after the firing began on Fort Sumter), he was offered command of the entire U.S. army! Again, he refused. He was fifty-four years old and he had never led troops in combat, but both sides recognized his extraordinary potential.

Then, on April 18, Virginia seceded. As far as Robert was concerned, that changed everything. The next day, he sat down and composed his letter of resignation. It was a brief, formal declaration that revealed none of the agony he felt after twenty-two years—twenty-six, including his cadet years at West Point—of unswerving devotion to the United States of America. But the die was cast. Mary wrote a friend, "My husband has wept tears of blood." On April 22, he accepted a commission as major general in command of the army and navy of Virginia.

Why did a highly decorated soldier for whom loyalty was a lifelong obsession renounce his oath of service, turn his back on his nation, and take up the rebel banner? As historians remind us, Robert "had no sympathy with either secession or slavery and, loving the Union and the army, deprecated the thought of sectional conflict." He told his son Custis, "I am not pleased with the course of the 'Cotton States' as they now term themselves....One of their plans seems to be the renewal of the slave trade. That I am opposed to on every ground." But he took a different tone with his sister Ann, an ardent Unionist: "I have not been able to make up my mind to raise my hands against my relatives, my children, my home." Loyalty to the "Old Dominion" of Virginia came first. He was also convinced, as were a majority of Southerners, that the "constitutional bond between the states" had been violated. If he had been in a position of influence, he would have seen to it that this violation was protested peacefully, but he was a soldier, not a politician. He presented his final thoughts on the matter to his family:

Secession is nothing but revolution....Still, a Union that can only be maintained by swords and bayonets, and in which strife and civil war are to take the place of brotherly love and kindness, has no charm for me. If the Union is dissolved, the government disrupted, I shall return to my native state and share the miseries of my people. Save in her defense, I will draw my sword no more.

He had never before delivered a public address; his first was in the rotunda of the Richmond capital building, where he accepted his commission in an elaborate formal ceremony that the new Confederate government insisted would be good publicity. Listeners were surely disappointed in their new leader's performance; Robert said very little, and what he did say was not inspirational. If they were looking for a firebrand to raise a rallying cry throughout the land, they would have to look elsewhere. He had embraced the southern cause with reluctance, and he was pessimistic about its chances for success. While all his peers were predicting a quick and decisive victory, Robert was certain that secession would lead to "a prolonged and bloody war." He estimated, in fact, that the conflict might last ten years. One southern war hawk objected: "He wishes to repress the enthusiasm of our people." And he was right.

Robert thought that Southerners were naïve about the nature of war and ill-prepared to face the great demands it would soon make upon them. Yet he rapidly and efficiently mobilized the militia and increased its size from 18,400 to 40,000 men to defend Virginia's more than 67,000 square miles of territory. He completed his task so well that the militiamen were almost immediately reclassified as Confederate regulars. Ironically, Robert became "a general without an army." Thus, when the Battle of Bull Run was fought on July 21, he was stuck in Richmond reading dispatches. Confederate President Jefferson Davis promised him that he would have a command soon, but in the meantime, he sent him to western (now West) Virginia to advise the troops fighting at Cheat Mountain (September 11–13) and at Gauley Bridge (November 1–10).

But what authority did an "advising" general have? Robert did not know, and no one else did either. He tried to coordinate attack strategies, emphasizing concentrated assaults, speed, and surprise, but the other generals dismissed most of his ideas. He similarly failed to convince them of the value of strict discipline among the troops. When he encountered a young lieutenant who casually inquired where he should procure a rifle and ammunition after having lazed about camp for a week, Robert lamented, "This is in keeping with everything else I find here—no order, no organization, nobody knows where anything is, no one understands his duty!"

Not surprisingly, the Confederates failed to dislodge Federal troops from western Virginia. Because he was at least nominally in charge, Robert was blamed by the press. A prominent editorialist complained, "The most remarkable circumstance of this campaign was that it was conducted by a general who had never fought a battle, who had a pious horror of guerrillas, and whose extreme tenderness of blood induced him to depend exclusively on the resources of strategy, to essay the achievement of victories without the cost of life." No doubt Robert was stung by such accusations, but he could take comfort in the fact that President Davis had faith in him and in the one instance of good fortune that he had enjoyed in western Virginia: He found a prime bit of horseflesh, a gray stallion that would serve as a perfect mount (as well as a best friend and even a lifesaver, as he would discover ere long). He paid two hundred dollars for the creature and named him Traveller.[4]

---

4   Probably the most famous horse in American history, with the possible exception of Man o' War, Traveller carried Lee through every battle from the Seven Days, Second Bull Run, Antietam, Fredericksburg, Chancellorsville, and Gettysburg to the Wilderness, Spotsylvania, Cold Harbor, Petersburg, Sayler's Creek, and Appomattox. He outlived Lee and was buried at Washington and Lee University. In 1907, his skeleton was disinterred and is now on display in the university's museum.

His next assignment was to establish strong coastal defenses in South Carolina, Georgia, and Florida, where a sea invasion was imminent. Robert arrived in November to find not only that Port Royal, South Carolina, had fallen, but also that disorder and confusion reigned everywhere. The local citizenry refused to offer any assistance to remedy the situation. He wrote to his daughter Mildred, "Another forlorn hope expedition. Worse than western Virginia." To his daughter Annie, "The people do not seem to realize that there is a war....[They] leave the protection of themselves & families to others." And to his son Custis, "They have all of a sudden realized the asperities of war, which they must encounter & do not seem prepared for it." With almost no money, supplies, or men, he could do little, though he spent every day in the saddle from morning till night conducting inspections and erecting what defenses were feasible with great energy and determination.

Charleston, South Carolina, was blockaded by Federal ships in December, and a great fire devastated the city.[5] In February of 1862, Roanoke, North Carolina, surrendered after a token battle. With the loss of two vital forts in Tennessee in the same month, the Confederacy appeared to be in deep trouble. In March of 1862, Davis recalled Robert to Virginia to help meet the greatest threat of all. Union Commander George McClellan was about to march on Richmond with a massive army of 100,000 men and another 45,000 in reserve. The timing couldn't have been worse. Enlistments were about to expire. Within a month or two, the Confederacy would be "a nation without an army."

At Robert's urging, General Thomas "Stonewall" Jackson rode north with his troops to create a diversion in the Shenandoah Valley. It worked magnificently, but only temporarily. Day by day, the Federals got closer to the capital. Confederate Commander Joseph E. Johnston tried to stop them at the Battle of Seven

---

[5] During the evacuation, Robert carried an infant to safety, and he was one of the first to donate money to a relief fund afterward.

Pines/Fair Oaks on May 31. Confederate casualties (killed, wounded, captured, and missing) numbered six thousand; the Federals lost five thousand. During the conflict, Johnston was badly injured, and Robert finally received his long-awaited battle command on June 1. He replaced Johnston as commanding general of the main Confederate army, which he promptly rechristened the Army of Northern Virginia.

In the next three years, he would become one of the greatest military commanders the world has ever seen. But, of course, no one knew that in 1862, Robert was a general on paper only. Combat was the testing ground that would prove his real worth. Deserved or not, his dismal record of failure in the first year of the war in western Virginia and along the east coast did not augur well for his success. Nor did his first official actions. He convinced the Confederate Congress to institute conscription, which was highly unpopular among Southerners who felt they were already fighting a war against precisely this kind of incursion on personal liberty. He purged his staff of those he felt were incompetent to lead, and totally reorganized the command structure of the army, making a number of powerful enemies in the process. He imposed strict discipline in camp and warned that deserters would be executed. And then he gave the order to "dig in." This was nonsense as far as the troops were concerned. They were impatient to "lick the Yanks," and they wanted to rush headlong into battle. They grumbled that their new commander was not acting like "General Lee" but "Granny Lee."

Why did a highly decorated soldier for whom loyalty was a lifelong obsession renounce his oath of service, turn his back on his nation, and take up the rebel banner?

If they had fought alongside him in the Mexican War fifteen years earlier, they might have better understood the importance of using the terrain to turn numerical disadvantages into strategic advantages. Or if they had been with him on the Mississippi River twenty-five years earlier, they might have understood his engineer's strategy; digging in would channel the enemy like a great river to flow into just the right place at just the right time where the defenders would have the upper hand. Robert could have explained to his detractors what was in his mind, but after the past year's experience, he suspected they wouldn't listen. He simply ordered them to keep at it with picks and shovels, and when they complained about the hard work, he chided, "There is nothing so military as labour & nothing so important to an army as to save the lives of its soldiers." The only one who seemed to have a clue about "Granny Lee's" true mettle was a staff aide named Joseph Christmas Ives. When another aide raised doubts about their commander's boldness, Ives replied that "if there is one man in either army, Federal or Confederate, who is, head & shoulders, far above every other one in either army for audacity that man is General Lee, and you will very soon have lived to see it. Lee is audacity personified." Here, in brief, was Robert's grand plan to thwart the invasion:

> Hold the Federals outside of Richmond with the defensive works the troops were now preparing. The better the earthworks, the fewer men it would require to keep McClellan at bay. With two-thirds of his army Lee proposed to attack the Federal right flank and drive the enemy from his works. And into the rear of McClellan's right flank Lee planned to unleash Jackson's Valley army following a rapid secret march from the Shenandoah.
>
> Here was ample audacity. If the Federals realized how thin were Lee's lines in front of Richmond, they could storm into the city, capture Lee's government, cut Lee's lines of supply and communication, and then watch Lee starve for a while on the Chickahominy bottom before receiving the surrender of his floundering army.

The Battle of Seven Days commenced on June 26 and lasted until July 2. Fortunately, McClellan was fooled into thinking the Confederates had 200,000 men instead of 92,000, so he moved his troops slowly and cautiously. But communications, weather, and travel problems (as well as his own fatigue) kept Jackson from flanking the Federals as planned. Confederate losses by the second day were running four times as high as those of the enemy. Day three, however, brought a sudden change of fortune. The Confederates achieved a great victory and by the next day had the Federals on the run. Days five and six should have been devoted to hot pursuit and the destruction of the retreating army, but Robert's division commanders didn't act swiftly enough. And the seventh day was "a gallant disaster." Robert ordered a frontal attack, but the infantry failed to mass. The brigades and divisions that did march piecemeal into the face of the Federal guns were mercilessly shot down.

The battle *was* a victory and proved Robert could be bold and daring. His men no longer called him "Granny Lee." He was now referred to admiringly as the "Gray Fox." But the Battle of Seven Days also revealed that he could not trust his subordinates to carry out orders or to improvise well on their own. There was little he could do about it, either. A new age had dawned. Battlefields were now measured "in miles not yards." A commander could not be everywhere at once; therefore, he had to depend on his generals. The Army of Northern Virginia boasted some of the most competent military leaders in American history, but it also had its share of incompetents. To compound the problem, even the most talented, experienced generals were prone to jealous in-fighting and insubordination.

Without hesitation, however, Robert went on the offensive after ending the immediate threat to Richmond. It was "the beginning of the *annus mirabilis,* the year of wonder, in Southern military fortunes." He was a genius at knowing where to strike; even his aides couldn't predict where he would move next. He seldom ordered frontal attacks in which his smaller numbers were a liability. Instead, he flanked the enemy by using the cavalry as bait to lure Federal troops into exposing their position. During many of the engagements, he rode up and down the lines, noting weaknesses and strengths, giving encouragement to the men. He "achieved amazing martial feats" and very nearly won the war that year. As one example, he dealt a stunning defeat to General John Pope at the Second Battle of Bull Run (August 29–30). This time, the Federals lost 14,500 to the Confederates' 9,500 casualties. During the battle, Robert divided his army and ordered a forced march through the mountains. But once again the opportunity to destroy the retreating army was squandered. His troops were simply too exhausted and, as he wrote in his report to Jefferson Davis, "they had nothing to eat for three days."

But the Army of Northern Virginia was checked by McClellan in Maryland in September. The Confederate battle plan, wrapped around a bundle of cigars carried by a secret courier, accidentally fell into Union hands. Robert was also handicapped because he had too few generals in the field. Those who were available were constantly quarreling. (One even arrested another, and Robert was forced to intervene.) And the army—whittled down to half-strength by casualties, disease, straggling, and desertions—was in the worst shape since the beginning of the war. Most of the "Johnny Rebs" were dressed in rags and were crippled by diarrhea that came from eating green corn, the only food they could find. A bystander wrote:

> When I say that they were hungry, I convey no impression of the gaunt starvation that looked from their cavernous eyes....I saw the troops march past us every summer for four years, and I know something of the appearance of a marching army...but never before or after did I see anything comparable to the demoralized state of the Confederates at this time. Never were want and exhaustion more visibly put before my eyes, and that they could march or fight at all seemed incredible.

But march and fight they did. They plunged straight into the Battle of Antietam and the "bloodiest single day of the entire war"—September 17, 1862. The Confederate force of 39,000

reported 1,546 killed, 7,754 wounded, and 1,018 missing. The
Federals, who had 71,500 men, reported 2,108 killed, 9,549
wounded, and 753 missing. Military historians question whether
Robert should have made a stand at Antietam; as one says, "he
very nearly lost his army and the war" then and there. But once
again, he managed to use his smaller force brilliantly and exploit
McClellan's chronic indecision and over caution.

The Maryland campaign was a "draw," but the North
claimed victory since it had halted the invasion. The Army of
Northern Virginia withdrew, taking solace from the great news
about the war in the West: The Army of Tennessee had seized
control of Kentucky. While his men cheered, Robert fretted. He
knew how fleeting such victories could be. He was not at all surprised when the rebels were forced back to Tennessee in October.
Meanwhile, he worked desperately to rebuild his own army. He
shrewdly guessed that the new Union commander, General Ambrose
Burnside, was about to attack Fredericksburg as a preliminary
move in a second attempt to invade Richmond. And that is
exactly what happened on December 13, 1862. Burnside, with
a force of 113,000, ordered six frontal attacks. Lee, who had
only 75,000 men and who once more had insisted that his soldiers "dig in," repulsed them all. With each attack, the Federals
had to charge across open, unprotected ground. As he witnessed the slaughter, Robert exclaimed with fierce emotion, "It is
well that war is so terrible, [lest] we should grow too fond of it!"
He had written to his wife on the same theme:

But what a cruel thing is war. To separate & destroy families &
friends & mar the purest joys & happiness God has granted us in
this world. To fill our hearts with hatred instead of love for our
neighbors & to devastate the fair face of this beautiful world.

There was a temporary truce on December 15 to bury the dead.
One of the witnesses recalled that everywhere there were

dead bodies... swollen to twice the natural size... lying in every conceivable posture—some on their backs with gaping jaws—some with eyes as large as walnuts, protruding with a glassy stare—some doubled up like a contortionist—here one without a head—there one without legs—yonder a head and legs without a trunk—everywhere horrible expressions—fear, rage, agony, madness, torture—lying in pools of blood—lying with heads half-buried in mud, with fragments of shell sticking in the oozing brain—with bullet holes all over the puffed limbs.

December 15, 1862
This was the terrible face of war. It was a face Robert had seen before and that he had never ceased to hate. The sight of it made his stomach turn and his knees shake. His heart went out to the men who lay dead and dying in the farm fields that had turned into killing fields at Fredericksburg. He thought that it was only poetic justice that their uniforms were now indistinguishable—you couldn't tell the blue from the gray because of all the dust, and mud, and blood. Were his sons out there? He'd had no word yet. Custis was on President Davis's staff, but he was sometimes sent on courier missions to the front lines. Rooney, who had been a cavalry officer under J. E. B. Stuart since the beginning of the war, was now a brigadier general. His horse had been shot out from under him at Cheat Mountain, but hopefully he still continued to evade death. Rob, the youngest, had left the University of Virginia and enlisted as a nineteen-year-old private in the Rockbridge Artillery last spring. Already, he'd risen to the rank of a lieutenant and was fighting with Rooney's outfit. And then there was his favorite nephew, Louis Marshall, who was fighting on the Union side, God bless him.

He whispered a feverent prayer for all of them, and he didn't forget to include his wife and daughters. They were in danger, too, since they were trapped behind enemy lines. He was especially concerned about Mary, his troublesome, headstrong, but ever lovable wife. Her imagined medical complaints had developed into a real disease, arthritis, and the doctors said she would soon be confined to a wheel-chair. He said another prayer for his daughter Annie. She had died of typhoid fever in October. Only twenty-three, she was. He had not seen her for two years, and he couldn't even get away long enough to attend her funeral. At times like this, he wished his body were lying in the fields. Then all his earthly cares would be over.

But then, as awful as things were, there was much for which he could be thankful. His men, for instance. They had been through such hard times, and yet they were still able to hold their heads high. Returning to the tent that served as his headquarters, he could hear their songs and laughter as they sat around campfires, cleaning their rifles, sorting through their kits, and preparing the evening meal. They'd done well here. They'd beaten the Yankees soundly and stopped the northern invasion in its tracks. And they had a little beef and bread to eat for a change. If Burnside ran true to form and withdrew to let his troops lick their wounds, they would also have a few days to rest up before the next fight. The war, for the moment, was on hold.

ROBERT WORRIED CONSTANTLY about his family and his troops, but he rarely regarded the danger to himself. He once wrote deprecatingly to Rooney's wife, Charlotte:

My coat is of gray, of the regulation style and pattern, and my pants of dark blue as is also prescribed, [hide] my long boots. I have the same handsome hat which surmounts my gray head (the latter not prescribed in the regulations) and shields my ugly face, which is masked by a white beard as stiff and as wiry as the teeth of a [cotton] card. In fact, an uglier person you have never seen, and so unattractive is it to our enemies that they shoot at it whenever visible to them....

On many occasions in battle, he deliberately put himself in harm's way. He argued that the men must be able to see that he was unafraid and that he shared their peril. But there was another eminently more practical reason for his actions, which he confessed to a young staff officer in a fiery fight near the end of the war. Robert had ridden to the top of a hill near the front to watch the firing of the batteries. The officer in question followed shortly with an important dispatch. Robert waited until the officer had performed his errand and then told him he must return by another less dangerous route; he had unnecessarily exposed himself by riding up the side of the hill that was closest to the enemy. The officer replied that he was ashamed to worry about his own safety when his commander "was sitting in plain view of the Federals." Robert answered shortly, "It is my duty to be here. I *must* see!"

In the midst of the Second Battle at Bull Run, he almost paid for this policy with his life when his cheek was grazed by a bullet. Upon returning to the company of his staff aides, who panicked at the sight of so much blood, he merely said matter-of-factly, "A Yankee sharpshooter came near to killing me just now." In March of 1863, Robert was struck down not by a bullet but by an unknown illness. He was bedridden for weeks and he continued to feel unwell through the fall. He had probably suffered from an attack of "angina pectoris," heart pain caused by a temporary lack of oxygen, and a much more serious ailment called "arteriosclerosis," an artery disease that could lead to a stroke.

But he did not know this. What he *did* know was that time was running out for the Confederacy. General Burnside had been replaced by Joseph Hooker, a much more aggressive and therefore deadlier foe. Once more outnumbered two to one, Robert managed to drive Hooker back at the Battle of Chancellorsville (May 2–4, 1863), his greatest victory, by dividing his small army and sending troops on a twelve-hour forced march to flank the Federal forces. Led by Stonewall Jackson, this detachment was detected by Hooker's scouts, who mistakenly assumed it was retreating. The Confederates then swept down on the unsuspecting Bluecoats while they were lounging in camp. It was a complete and utter rout. The Federal army was in total disarray and ripe for destruction. At the conclusion of the three-day battle, one of Robert's staff recalled:

> One long, unbroken cheer, in which the feeble cry of those who lay helpless on the earth blended with the strong voices of those who still fought, rose high above the roar of battle and hailed the presence of the victorious chief. He sat in the full realization of all that soldiers dream of—triumph; and as I looked upon him in the complete fruition of the success...I thought that it must have been from such a scene that men in ancient days rose to the dignity of gods.

Frustratingly, once more the Confederates were unable to catch the Federals as they fled across the Rappahannock. And, worst of all, Robert's ablest lieutenant, Jackson, was mortally wounded by friendly fire.

Like a ship tossed from one wave to another in a stormy sea, the Confederacy seemed to teeter on the brink of collapse, then on the brink of victory, and then on the brink of collapse again. Just days after Chancellorsville, Robert received the alarming news that Union General Ulysses S. Grant was about to capture one of the crown jewels of the South—Vicksburg, Mississippi. He lost no time, therefore, in setting out for Pennsylvania to fight this new threat by carrying the war into the enemy's territory. At the same time, he wrote a long epistle to President Davis, imploring him to consider the peace overtures that were being offered by the North.

As every schoolchild knows (or used to know, when history was properly taught), Robert's invasion attempt resulted in the disastrous Confederate defeat at the Battle of Gettysburg. Whole books have been written about this single engagement. It overshadows not only the history of the Civil War but the history of warfare. In large part, it is the valor of the combatants that is responsible. Heroes were in plentiful supply at Gettysburg, and their stories are legion. There was also the suspenseful way the battle proceeded from Seminary Ridge to Culp's Hill, to the Devil's Den and Little Round Top, and finally Cemetery Ridge— places that have since become hallowed ground. And, of course, there was the clash of two centuries: At Gettysburg, cavalry officers with sabers flying—like ghosts of the Napoleonic era—rode straight into the slaughterhouse of modern artillery and rifles that would soon be used with deadly force in two world wars.[6]

Arguably, there is another even more compelling reason for continuing interest in this battle: We want to know, did Robert E. Lee blunder? In other words, did he make a fatal mistake by going on the offensive and invading Pennsylvania? Did he break his cardinal rule about not letting the enemy pick the time or the place to fight? And once the battle had commenced, was his heart condition responsible for his bad decisions or was he simply too stubborn to change tactics? It was true that invading Pennsylvania seemed foolhardy. But Robert was persuaded that all was lost

---

[6] Actually, this romantic image, for all its enduring popularity, is not strictly accurate. There was only one saber charge, and it was led by Federal cavalry. Moreover, troops on both sides were armed the same way and fought the same way. Most were still using the old muzzle-loading rifles and muskets which, at best, had a range of a few hundred yards. Some had Henry and Spencer repeating rifles. As with practically all the battles fought during the Civil War, at Gettysburg, the defenders had the greatest advantage.

unless he took the risk. Unlike Jefferson Davis and the rest of the Confederacy's leaders, he did not believe that this war would be like the American Revolution. Simply keeping the rebel army alive and outlasting the enemy would not work this time. The Yankees were not the Redcoats. They would not get tired of fighting and go home. They would keep coming, and in greater numbers. They already had far more men, more money, more food, more weapons. This was a war of attrition, and it was only a matter of time before the South's limited resources were totally exhausted. A quick and decisive victory—a "showdown," according to one of his biographers—was what Robert was looking for.

As to the issue of where and when the battle was fought, he did act precipitously. But then his cavalry commander, General J. E. B. Stuart, was off on a raid. There was no proper reconnaissance, and no one realized that the Army of the Potomac was on the move in late June of 1863.[7] But Robert did learn on June 28 that George Meade had ascended to the post of commanding general. He felt Meade would advance much more quickly than his predecessors, so taking the initiative and making a first strike, even under adverse conditions, seemed imperative.

> Robert told his son Custis, "I am not pleased with the course of the 'Cotton States' as they now term themselves....One of their plans seems to be the renewal of the slave trade. That I am opposed to on every ground."

The legendary leader of the Army of Northern Virginia arrived at the sleepy little town of Gettysburg on the afternoon of July 1. Along his route, he heard cannon fire and knew a battle had begun before his army had had a chance to assemble in force. He was no doubt disturbed that he had still had no word from Stuart about Federal troop movements. He decided to send word for all his men to converge on Gettysburg as quickly as possible. That evening, after a full day's fighting, he directed General Richard Ewell to launch an assault on a small

---

7   Historians disagree about whether Stuart is to blame for this; the orders he received were vague.

Federal contingent that was occupying the best high ground in the area, a gently rolling, grassy knoll known as Cemetery Hill. Ewell decided it was too risky, however, and before long, the Federals were occupying the hill in great numbers.[8] Lee was no doubt furious with Ewell, but he did not dwell upon his anger. He instructed his "old war horse," General James Longstreet, to take the commanding heights on the following morning before Meade could arrive with his main army. Longstreet feared that his commander was making a major strategic mistake by not fighting a defensive battle as he had at Fredericksburg. There is strong evidence to suggest that he was correct in this assumption.[9] Robert was simply too anxious to force a speedy conclusion to the war. Longstreet moved incredibly slowly and did not follow orders until six o'clock in the evening. This meant that other vital assaults on Culp's Hill and the Round Tops, which would have been virtually unopposed in the morning, had to be delayed. By the time Longstreet's men did attack, they faced a formidable enemy and the fighting became intense and bloody.

From his headquarters on Seminary Ridge, Robert could not see much of what was happening, but he believed that the battle was going badly only because his generals would not coordinate their attacks. Though he was reportedly ill, there is no evidence that his judgment was clouded. On July 3, Longstreet, convinced (again, correctly) that an offensive would be tantamount to suicide, argued against a massed assault on Cemetery Ridge. But Robert felt that it was the only alternative. "Pickett's Charge" of fifteen thousand men, led by General George E. Pickett, lasted barely an

8 Once more, there is unceasing debate about whether such an assault would have succeeded had it been launched much earlier.

9 After the war, Longstreet continued to maintain that the defeat at Gettysburg was Robert E. Lee's fault. He was joined in this opinion by a number of other generals who said that it was at this point that their faith in the "Gray Fox" was shaken. Others, like General Jubal Early, the leading proponent of the "Lost Cause" school, stood steadfast by their commander and claimed that Gettysburg would have yielded victory if the battle plan had been carried out as conceived.

hour. Once again, Longstreet failed to provide the covering support Robert requested.[10] No one knows if that support would have made a difference, but Pickett's Charge was Fredericksburg all over again. This time, however, it was the men in gray who were met with a withering barrage of artillery and rifle fire under the blistering sun. One of the soldiers who survived the ordeal recaptured the feelings of desperation and terror:

> Directly in front of us, breathing flame in our very faces, the long range of the guns which must be taken thunder on our quivering melting ranks....The line becomes unsteady because at every step a gap must be closed....Our men are falling faster now, for the deadly musket is at work. Volley after volley of crushing musket balls sweeps through the line and mows us down like wheat before the scythe.
>
> On! On men! Thirty yards more...but who can stand such a storm of hissing lead and iron?

By any standards, Gettysburg was a debacle. Confederate casualties exceeded twenty thousand. Many soldiers deserted afterward. Robert took full responsibility and refused to blame Stuart, Ewell, Longstreet, or anyone else. He even offered to resign, but President Davis refused to relieve him.[11]

---

[10] Was such support even available? It is difficult to say. Longstreet had only one fresh division—Pickett's—to call upon. An added problem was that the Confederate artillery bombardment, one of the heaviest ever, completely failed to soften the Federal line. In the 1860s, cannons lacked accuracy and shells lacked explosive power. They were more effective weapons of defense, which is why the Federal artillery bombardment that followed was far more devastating.

[11] As one military historian points out, there are many arguments for and against Robert's greatness as a general. We should not make the mistake of critics who claim that as a military genius he was a sham, or fans who claim he was infallible and who tolerate no criticism of his tactics on the battlefield. Nor should we forget that it was his personal character that was the source of his true greatness. Great generals come and go. The Civil War boasted several of them, including Stonewall Jackson and Robert's nemesis, Ulysses S. Grant. But great leaders of men, such as Robert E. Lee, are rare indeed.

It was now, without question, a defensive war. In March of 1864, Ulysses S. Grant was appointed commander of all the Union armies. Here was a new adversary, brilliant, determined, and "ruthless" in the eyes of Southerners. Robert feared that he would be unstoppable. There would be no major battles until May, when Grant moved against Richmond in the Wilderness Campaign, yet for those two months a feeling of desperation gripped the South.

May 6, 1864

It was 5:00 A.M. Robert was up and pacing in front of his tent in the northern Virginia tangle of woods and swamps known as "the Wilderness," waiting for sunrise to show him what the enemy was up to. Grant had 120,000 men. He had only 60,000, and some of them had not yet come up from the rear. He gave a rueful smile as he slipped on his gloves and mounted Traveller. Some things never changed. He couldn't remember not being outnumbered or outgunned. He would make do, as always, with what he had.

Suddenly, a great clap of thunder rang in his ears. No, not thunder. It was artillery fire. Instinctively, he realized what must be happening. The Federals were attacking the gap between General Hill's and General Ewell's lines. Longstreet was supposed to have arrived at midnight to close the gap, but he must have fallen behind. All was in confusion. The men, who were chopping timber and digging trenches, dropped their tools and ran pell-mell for the rear. Robert wheeled Traveller around and stopped in the middle of the road, trying to turn them. He hailed one officer, "General McGowan, is this splendid brigade of yours running like a flock of geese?"

"General, these men are not whipped. They only want a place to form, and they will fight as well as they ever did."

But nothing could halt the panicking soldiers. In a few minutes, the Federals would overrun and capture all the Confederate guns. Robert ordered the colonel in charge to fire one last desperate volley. Then, peering through the choking, blinding smoke, he saw a group of soldiers (the overdue reinforcements from Longstreet) fighting their way through the retreating horde toward the battle.

"Who are you, my boys?" he shouted.

"Texas boys, sir!"

"Hurrah for Texas!" Robert shouted with uncharacteristic exuberance as he waved his hat wildly, "Hurrah for Texas!"

Quickly he formed them into line and would have led them into battle but for one of his aides who grabbed Traveller's bridle.

"Go back, General Lee, go back! We won't go unless you go back!" the Texans cried.

He remembered their words as the Wilderness Campaign segued right into the Spotsylvania Campaign and the infamous Battle of the Bloody Angle on May 12. Here, thought Robert, as he witnessed the frenzied fighting with awe and horror, was Pickett's charge at Gettysburg lasting all day. Mortar shells literally felled giant oaks. Infantrymen fought with rifles, bayonets, pikes, and knives. A light rain began to fall, but those locked in combat barely seemed to notice.

At one point, the Federals launched a massive assault on a weak point in the Confederates' seven-and-a-half mile trench system. The defenders scattered, just as they had done in the Wilderness. Hundreds of demoralized soldiers streamed past Robert. His voice was as deep as the growl of a tempest as he said: "Shame on you, men, shame on you! Go back to your regiments!"

They cried back, "We can't hold them! It can't be done!" and kept on running.

Robert did not heed their excuses. He turned Traveller's head in the direction of the advancing enemy. He was going to lead a charge with such men as would follow him, or perish in the effort.

One of his commanders, General John B. Gordon, spurred his horse and blocked Traveller's path. In a voice that he hoped might reach the ears of his men, he called out, "General Lee, you shall not lead my men in a charge. No man can do that, sir. Another is here for that purpose. These men behind you are Georgians, Virginians, and Carolinians. They have never failed you on any field. They will not fail you here. Will you, boys?"

The response came like a mighty anthem. "No, no, no; we'll not fail him!"

Gordon then shouted, "General Lee, you must go to the rear!"

The echo, "General Lee to the rear, General Lee to the rear!" rolled back from the throats of the men, and they gathered around him to turn his horse in the opposite direction, some clutching his bridle, some his stirrups, some pressing close to old Traveller's withers, ready to shove him by main force to the rear.

Overcome, Robert barely managed to choke out the words, "If you will promise to drive those people from our works, I will go back!" And the rebel yells reverberated through the clearing.

THE CONFEDERATES PUSHED the Federals back and shored up their position at the Bloody Angle. Twice in the same day, Robert tried to lead a charge, but his own soldiers refused to allow it. The men loved him with a fierce devotion that was beyond description. (Stonewall Jackson once expressed the sentiment of most of the officers and the rank and file: "I would follow him blindfold.") Robert had instigated the institution of the draft. He had imposed the death penalty for desertion. He could not pay his men or even feed or clothe them adequately. He had led them to shattering defeat at Gettysburg. But still they clung to him. Partly, this was because of his own personal brand of charisma. But it was also because he set an example they admired. He was

the man who could still smile, who was selfless in his compassion for others, the old gray warrior in the armor of a shining heart.

Everyone knew the hardships he bore, the despair he suffered, the tragedy he foresaw in the misery of his soul; yet he was the general who could get down from Traveller on a cold November morning and say to a flush-faced lieutenant: "My boy, let me show you how to build a fire...."

With his calmness, his composure, there grew this depth of good nature....Soldiers in the trenches...knew Lee best....Any tattered private could approach him without hesitancy or embarrassment; he was one of them, had grown old in the bitter struggle with them....

He ate the same food, slept in a tent, rarely took leaves, and toured the camps regularly. He showed courage in battle and took great personal risks. He also took pains to tell his followers how much he admired *them*. In his sincere opinion, they were the most magnificent and bravest fighting men he had ever seen. It was natural that they wanted to live up to his image of them. The single greatest factor that kept the South going, said one historian, was "trust in Robert E. Lee." Even in the darkest days of the war, Southerners still believed that their "George Washington" and his "Continental Army" would prevail.

At the Battle of Cold Harbor on June 3, the Confederates inflicted heavy casualties on Grant's divisions and won a signal victory. But the course of the war was shifting once more near the end of 1864. President Abraham Lincoln was reelected, which appeared to be a harbinger of four more years of war. Grant's forces trapped Lee's at Petersburg, Virginia, which threatened the entire southern rail network and Confederate supply lines. Union General Phil Sheridan soundly trounced Jubal Early's troops at Cedar Creek, Virginia. The Army of Tennessee was smashed in a battle at Franklin, Tennessee. And Union General William Tecumseh Sherman began his long "march to the sea" after burning a section of Atlanta. His troops pursued "total war," destroying supply lines, hounding the Confederate army, and making war on the civilian population. After all this, it seemed like adding insult to injury when on January 31, 1865, the Confederate Congress confirmed Robert as general-in-chief of all the rebel armies. There was great pressure for him to move his operations westward, but he continued to lead the Army of Northern Virginia as he had always done.

On April 2, 1865, Petersburg and Richmond finally fell after a brutal nine-month siege, and Robert was forced to beat a hasty nighttime retreat with his weary, starving men. When they lost their way in the dark, he positioned himself in the middle of a crossroads and directed traffic for hour after hour. But on April 4, when everyone finally made it safely to the appointed rendezvous, Amelia Court House, it was discovered that the promised rations had not arrived. As Robert pondered his options (none of which were agreeable) in the face of this calamity and waited for his men to return from foraging for provisions on April 5, his son Rooney arrived to warn that Sheridan's cavalry and Federal infantry were fast approaching. Now there was only one option: an all-night march to the town of Farmville where there was food and an opportunity to throw up fortifications. But the Confederates didn't get far, only to Sayler's Creek on April 6, before they were overtaken.

It was here, on a mild spring afternoon, that Robert watched helplessly as the Army of Northern Virginia was decimated. He had fled Petersburg with fewer than 30,000 men; now he was down to 22,000. Still, he refused to surrender. He gathered up the ragged remnant and led the way to Farmville. Once again, the food and supplies he expected were inexplicably missing. There was a final skirmish at dawn near Appomattox Station, but the odds were too great. Robert had fewer than 10,000 men in his command now, and they were utterly spent. He called his aides and said grimly, "Then there is nothing left me but to go and see General Grant, and I would rather die a thousand deaths." On Palm Sunday, April 9, 1865, he surrendered to Grant at the Appomatox Court House. As he left the building and rode away on the long-suffering Traveller, his distraught followers wept openly. One shouted, "I love you just as well as ever, General Lee."

Robert's last, poignant words to them were:

> Boys, I have done the best I could for you. Go home now, and if you will make as good citizens as you have soldiers, you will do well, and I shall always be proud of you. Good-bye and God bless you all.

"Surrender," said one perceptive observer, "is death raised to an enormous power." Robert was relieved that the war was over, but he could not be relieved by the way in which the deed had been accomplished. He "would need to grieve a long time." He also had to confront his own peculiar and perilous situation. He was not a free man. He was a paroled prisoner of war. After the strongest advocate of a conciliating peace, Abraham Lincoln, died on April 15, the victim of a pro-Confederate assassin, there was every possibility that Robert would be tried for treason.[12] He applied to President Andrew Johnson for amnesty, but his petition was "lost" in the bureaucratic shuffle.[13] Finally, Grant threatened to resign

---

[12] His U.S. citizenship was revoked for 110 years. On August 5, 1975, President Gerald Ford signed an act that granted Robert a full pardon—shortly after his lost Amnesty Oath finally surfaced in the State Department's archives!

[13] A federal judge in Norfolk, Virginia, unsuccessfully attempted to convince a grand jury to indict him on this charge.

unless Johnson exempted Robert from trial. Still, Northerners called him a monster. Southerners responded by calling him a martyr. Both appellations disturbed him, and he attempted to withdraw, unsuccessfully, from the public eye. Mercifully, his sons had survived, but the war years had brought about the death of his daughter Annie, his daughter-in-law Charlotte, and his only grandchildren, both of whom failed to survive infancy. Robert felt their loss keenly. In addition, he was nearly a pauper. The estate Mary had inherited from her parents and which had been the Lee's only permanent residence was seized by Union troops during the war. In an act of vengeance, the North made it the site of the Arlington National Cemetery, so that the "Gray Fox" might never go home again. Now homeless and practically penniless, Robert knew he would have to find a way to earn a living, but he didn't know how he would be able to do so in the present situation.

After his return to Richmond in June, he went to Mass one day at St. Paul's Episcopal Church. (He had been unchurched until age forty-six, when he was confirmed with his daughters Mary and Annie. Since then, he had found great comfort in the Scriptures and in attending religious services.) The membership rolls of St. Paul's "read like a *Who's Who* of the Confederacy." When the minister called for the congregation to approach and receive communion,

a tall, well-dressed, and very black man stood and strode to the rail. There followed a pregnant pause. According to one witness, "Its effect upon the communicants was quite startling, and for several moments they retained their seats in solemn silence and did not move, being deeply chagrined by this attempt to inaugurate the 'new regime' to offend and humiliate them...."

Then another person rose from the pew and walked down the aisle to the chancel rail. He knelt near the black man and so redeemed the circumstance. This grace-bringer, of course, was Robert E. Lee. Soon after he knelt, the rest of the congregation followed his example and shuffled in turn to the rail.

It was a defining moment in Robert E. Lee's life and a defining moment in the life of the South. Healing *would* come, if it were sought in the spirit of Christian charity and forgiveness.

Not long after that, in August of 1865, a friend of Robert's came calling to inform him he had been unanimously elected president of a college in Lexington, Virginia. Someday this premier educational institution would be known as Washington and Lee University, but for now it was just Washington College. Robert apologized profusely; he was gratified by the offer, but he had never heard of the place. The friend explained that although it was an obscure little school, it had great potential. Robert replied that he would consider the invitation and let him know his answer shortly. In the meantime, he received several far more attractive offers from the University of the South in Sewanee, Tennessee, and the University of Virginia. But the more he thought about it, the more Washington College appealed to him. It would be a fresh start. And although he had been too restless to enjoy teaching and administrating at West Point, he was at a stage in his life where these duties seemed rewarding and fulfilling. They might even help him find a way to build bridges between the North and South, which was his new (and secret) mission in life.

After he had vouchsafed his acceptance, he packed his bags, saddled Traveller, and rode four days alone to the campus, which he had never seen. He arrived on September 18, 1865, wearing an old woolen suit and a battered hat. He insisted on a simple inauguration ceremony with no fanfare. After taking his oath, he "walked to his office and went to work." Once again in his turbulent life, he faced a daunting challenge. The bleak condition of Washington College was best described by his son Rob:

> Its buildings, library, and apparatus had suffered from the sack and plunder of hostile soldiers. Its invested funds, owing to the general impoverishment throughout the land, were for the time being rendered unproductive and their ultimate value was most uncertain.

Four professors still remained on duty, and there were about forty students, mainly from the country around Lexington....It was very poor, indifferently equipped with buildings, and with no means in sight to improve its condition.

Robert knew that the trustees wanted a famous figurehead only to raise money for the school, but he was determined to do much more. He expanded the curriculum and hired more professors. He sought to establish good relations between the local community and the college. And he encouraged Northerners to apply for admission. On top of all this, he carried on a huge correspondence and acted as a mentor to students, especially troublesome ones. He steadfastly avoided politics and refused the nomination for the governorship of Virginia. In May of 1868, he stopped a lynching in progress, and he did much in his quiet but authoritative way to improve race relations in the local community. In defeat, he was at last discovering a life of ultimate victory. He might have retreated completely from society, but he didn't. He continued, as he always had, to maintain a positive outlook on life. He once wrote to Custis when the latter was just a young cadet having trouble at West Point:

Shake off those gloomy feelings. Drive them away....All is bright if you will think it so. All is happy if you will make it so....Live in the world you inhabit. Look upon things as they are. Take them as you find them. Make the best of them. Turn them to your advantage.

He admitted that sadness and tragedy "will sometimes come over us....They are the shadows to our picture. They bring out prominently the light & the bright spots. They must not cover up *all*. They must not *hide* the picture itself." They must be regarded "as a medium through which to view life correctly."

On September 27, 1870, he came home from a very long and fractious church vestry meeting. It was held in a damp, unheated room where members quarreled over various issues, including how to clear a $55 deficit. After more than three hours in which he hadn't spoken word, Robert said, "I will give that sum." He picked up his hat and his cloak and walked home in the pouring rain to the modest president's residence on the edge of campus. When he arrived, he was in such a weakened state that he could not speak. The sword of Damocles that had been hovering over him since he had first taken ill during the war had finally fallen; he suffered a massive stroke. He died a few days later, on October 12, at age sixty-three. After his passing, his daughter Mildred remarked in a line that made a fitting epitaph to the life of Robert E. Lee: "To me, he seems a Hero—& all other men small in comparison."

SUGGESTED READINGS

There are two rival interpretations of Lee. The "heroic" interpretation is presented by Douglas Southall Freeman in four Pulitzer Prize-winning volumes, *R.E. Lee: A Biography* (New York: Charles Scribner's Sons, 1934–35; abridged version, 1961). The harsher "revisionist" interpretation is presented by Thomas Connelly in *The Marble Man: Robert E. Lee and His Image in American Society* [1977] (Louisiana State University Press, 1978). Notably, a third interpretation, which masterfully attempts to reconcile the legend and the real man, was recently produced by Emory M. Thomas in *Robert E. Lee: A Biography* (New York: W.W. Norton & Company, 1995). Other excellent sources include: Earl Schenck Miers, *Robert E. Lee* (New York: Vintage Books, 1956); James K. Fitzpatrick, *Builders of the American Dream* (New Rochelle, N.Y.: Arlington House, 1977); and Gary W. Gallagher, Ed., *Lee: The Soldier* (Lincoln: University of Nebraska Press, 1996).

I am also particularly indebted to two distinguished Civil War historians, Albert Castel (Lincoln Prize-winning author of *The Decision in the West: The Atlanta Campaign of 1864* and many other fine books) and Arlan Gilbert (Hillsdale College professor and author of three excellent volumes on the college's history), for their editorial assistance in preparing this chapter. Their generosity and expertise made the difference.

Andrew Carnegie
Businessman and Philanthropist

(1835–1919)

The old nations of the earth keep on at a snail's pace. The Republic thunders past with the rush of the express train.

—Andrew Carnegie
Triumphant Democracy

April 1876

Hugh Miller, an accountant at the Edgar Thomson Steel Works, was greatly annoyed. He had just been interrupted, right in the middle of checking the quarterly balance sheets, by an officious junior clerk who had sailed into his office without so much as a by-your-leave saying that Superintendent Shinn wanted him to conduct a tour "right this minute for a very special visitor." Hugh was skeptical about the designation; "very special" probably meant second cousin by marriage to someone who knew someone on the board of directors. He was stuck with the chore because he was new to the firm, having only been on the job for about three weeks. Oh well, he said to himself as he removed his sleeve protectors and eyeshade and shrugged on his coat, it would be a chance to get out of the office for awhile.

He entered the visitor's waiting room. No one was there. He searched the halls. Then he peered outside the entrance to the main building. Hugh scratched his head and wondered, where on earth could the fellow be? He was about to give up and return to his work when, in the railyard that ran straight through the middle of the plant, he spied a tiny, old man in a dusty black suit and a bowler hat. He was talking animatedly with the workmen who were busy dumping coal from boxcars into long, tin-roofed sheds where it would be stored until it could be burned down to pure coke, the fuel needed to fire the blast furnaces.

"You're a rare one, sir," one of the workmen was saying with a grin to the stranger as Hugh approached.

The man's wide-set, blue eyes twinkled and his laugh was like the tinkling of a silver bell. Hugh was also amused, but for a different reason. Superintendent Shinn had not been exaggerating about a "very special visitor";

except for his somber attire, this was surely Saint Nicholas in the flesh. About fifty years of age, he stood only a little over five feet tall. He had a snowy white beard, ruddy cheeks, and a genial expression. When he spoke it was with a mild Scottish burr.

"So, you would be Hugh Miller, I reckon?"

"Yes, sir, I am, and you would be...?"

"Oh, just call me Andra, m' boy. No need to stand on formality, especially among fellow Scots, is there?"

Hugh was born in America and had no accent to betray his origins, but it was true his mother had been an Edinburgh lass. He wondered how the old gentleman knew. It was growing late, so, without further speculation, he took his charge by the arm and steered him gently but firmly toward the rail mill, which was the first stop in a sprawling complex of huge brick buildings, furnaces, and smokestacks along the banks of the Monongahela River a dozen miles outside of Pittsburgh. Raising his voice over the constant roar of the heavy machinery, he began his recitation: "The Edgar Thomson Steel Works was built between 1873 and 1875 by the famous industrialist Andrew Carnegie and his associates. No expense was spared in construction or design. See that?" He pointed up to the sky where the open-topped housing of the rail mill was barely visible. "There are steel plates and four-inch square bolts up there. This is the only facility in America built to such exacting specifications."

He went on, warming to his theme, "In fact, Edgar Thomson is widely hailed as the finest steel works in the nation. We have our own rail line, two five-ton Bessemer converter furnaces, two five-ton Siemens open hearth furnaces, a rolling mill, a gas works, a boiler department, a machine shop, a forge, an electric tram over the boilers and producers, and a waterworks. We're totally self-sufficient."

"*Magnificent!*" *the visitor exclaimed.* "*But tell me more about the two kinds of furnaces you mentioned. I don't believe I have ever heard of either of them.*"

"*I can do better than that,*" *Hugh smiled.* "*I'll show them to you.*" *They walked to one of the other buildings nearby.* "*The first kind of furnace you are going to see is named after its inventor, an Englishman named Henry Bessemer. In 1856, he discovered how to make steel from pig iron—that's the raw metal extracted from iron ore that has had some of the impurities removed and other elements added—by heating it to a high temperature and then adding cold air.*"

They came to a halt in front of one of the giant, pear-shaped converters.

"*It looks like a great metal beast!*" *Andra was awestruck.*

"*That's just what it is.*" *Hugh confirmed.* "*It is a dragon that breathes fire. Just watch.*"

He motioned to indicate where cold air was being forced through pipes into the lower end of the converter, which held molten pig iron, manganese, silicon, and car-bon. Even standing many feet away, Hugh and the visitor could feel the heat increase tremendously as the elements collided. Suddenly, a roaring flame came rushing from the mouth of the converter. In a matter of seconds, the flame turned deep violet, then burnt orange, then pure white. Several workmen stepped up to the platform and tapped the converter. A shining river of steel poured out into a giant ladle and then into waiting molds.[1]

"*Aye, that was magnificent,*" *Andra repeated the same encomium with a delighted clap of his hands.* "*What happens now?*"

---

[1] I am indebted to Joseph Frazier Wall, who is listed in the reading at the end of the chapter, for certain phrases in this description of the Bessemer process.

Hugh, once more the pedant, said, "When they are cooled, these ingots will be reheated and rolled into what we call 'blooms.' Then, the blooms are cut into 'billets' and rerolled into the finished product—in this case, steel rails. Now, let's move on."

They walked a few hundred yards to another immense brick building. "In here," Hugh said, "is a Siemens furnace, which works on an entirely different principle. It was invented by a German mechanic in 1861, and it produces the best steel in the world. Unfortunately, for many years it could process only high grade ore with a low phosphorus content, so it wasn't profitable to build. But, with recent technological improvements and the discovery of huge, low-phosphorus ore fields in the Mesabi Range in Minnesota, we can get around this problem and make production more economical. The two Siemens furnaces at this plant are the first in Pittsburgh and among the first in all of America. Everybody and his uncle declared that Mr. Carnegie was mad to spend so much on them, especially since the whole country is suffering because of the depression. But the old man's having the last laugh now; Edgar Thomson is currently producing more than thirty thousand tons of steel rails annually at a cost of $69 a ton.[2] Keep in mind, please, that it costs other firms $110 a ton to produce the same amount."

"Such a business! I can hardly comprehend it."

Andra's tone became brisk and businesslike. "Well, I thank you verra much for your time, young man. I'll be off now and leave you to get back to your work. Please give Superintendent Shinn my warmest regards."

Hugh was surprised that their parting was so abrupt; visitors usually demanded tea and sandwiches after a tour.

---

2   These were estimates quoted in an early projected financial statement. The real figures—both for tonnage produced and production costs—were probably higher. Incredibly, the Edgar Thomson plant paid for itself after just one year of production.

But, since he was anxious to return to his work, he simply shook the man's hand without protest and showed him to the main gate. Superintendent Shinn was waiting in his office when he returned.

"So, how did you like meeting the grand old man?"

"You mean Andra?" Hugh asked. "I suppose he was all right. A bit ignorant when it comes to understanding steelmaking, but then most people are."

"Andrew Carnegie ignorant about steelmaking?" his boss roared with laughter. "I doubt there's a man alive who knows more about the whole process, from mining the ore to selling the finished product on the market."

"You don't mean to tell me that Mr. Carnegie goes about taking tours of his own steel works?"

"Of course he does. He wants to see with his own eyes what's going on, and believe me, those innocent baby blues don't miss a trick. He particularly enjoys having bright young geniuses such as yourself conduct him around while he plays dumb—it's how he learns how much you know about the business."

Hugh gulped, "Do you think I passed the test?"

"Don't worry, I'm sure you did just fine. But you might want to prepare for his next visit. Then he'll grill you proper with questions like: 'Is your lime 48 or 50 percent of the mixture?' or 'What is your cost of labor per ton?' He likes the management staff to know about every aspect of the business. He can be a demanding taskmaster sometimes, but one thing is sure: Andrew Carnegie never asks more of others than he asks of himself. Since he was a boy, he has had to make his own way in the world, and he feels everyone else should, too."

ANDREW CARNEGIE, who was known to his family and friends as "Andra," or "Andy," was America's most famous businessman-turned-philanthropist. He was born on November 25, 1835, in Dunfermline, Scotland, a small town near the capital city of Edinburgh. His father, William, was a skilled weaver of fine damask linen who owned four looms and employed three apprentices. His mother, Margaret, was the daughter of a cobbler. She kept house and raised Andrew and his younger brother, Tom, who was born in 1843.[3] The Carnegies were a fiercely independent-minded, intellectual family. They read newspapers and books and debated the issues of the day with relatives and neighbors. They were active in the Chartist movement, which had spread from town to town in Scotland since 1837. Chartists subscribed to the "People's Charter" demanding the vote for laborers, voting by ballot, the abolition of property qualifications for membership in Parliament, annual Parliaments, and equal electoral districts. It would be half a century before most of these aims were achieved, but they had a powerful impact on young Andrew, who would grow up to be a champion of the working man.

At age eight, he entered a private school. His parents had already taught him to read, and he was soon recognized as one of the brightest students. He might have gone on to attend a university someday, but then something happened that would change his life forever. In 1847, a weaving factory with dozens of powerful, steam-driven looms opened in Dunfermline. As a historian records, "This was the Machine come at last to the linen industry. The gray smoke that poured out of the factory's chimneys to float over the town was the pennant of victory of the Machine over the Weaver, and everyone knew it." Over four hundred weavers traded in their hand looms for jobs in the factory, but William was one of the stubborn holdouts who refused to give up on the

---

3   A younger sister, Ann, died in infancy when Andrew was about four years old.

traditional way of doing things. But his linen was far more expensive than the mass-produced variety, and before long he could find no more buyers. For the first time, the Carnegie family knew hunger and deprivation. Andrew later wrote in his autobiography:

> The first serious lesson of my life came to me one day when he [William] had taken in the last of his work to the merchant, and returned to our little home greatly distressed because there was no more work for him to do. I was then just about ten years of age, but the lesson burned into my heart, and I resolved then that the wolf of poverty should be driven from our door someday, if I could do it.

A GREAT FINANCIAL DEPRESSION, which had begun in the early part of the decade, made matters even worse. Hundreds of workers, not just in the linen industry but in every industry, were being displaced by efficient machines. In time, this would be a great blessing, making more goods affordable, but for now, there was only confusion and anger among the laboring classes. Weavers in some towns dressed in disguise and burned the power looms that had put them out of business. The threat of revolution hung heavy over the nation, and the government began to clamp down on any activity that might promote further unrest. Andrew wrote as an old man, "I remember as if it were yesterday, being awakened during the night by a tap at the back window by men who had come to inform my parents that my uncle, Bailie Morrison, had been thrown in jail because he had dared to hold a meeting which had been forbidden."

Margaret, who was the practical-minded member of the family, pointed out that they might all end up in jail or they might starve, like those in Ireland and western Scotland who were dying because of the potato famine, which had begun in 1845 as a result of crop failure. She had two sisters who had emigrated to America. They should sell their meager property, borrow some funds from relatives, and move to the New World. It was their only hope. After a long delay, William finally agreed, and they made plans to leave their beloved home in Dunfermline. The night before their ship sailed, William sat alone in the main room of the family cottage staring at the empty space where his looms once proudly stood. There was a knock on the door. He went to answer it and found one of his sisters there with tears in her eyes. She pressed all the wealth she had—two pounds and ten shillings—into his hands and wished him Godspeed. He was overcome by her gesture, but at age forty-three, he could summon no optimism. He was tired and disillusioned. For young Andrew, on the other hand, the move to America signaled high adventure. He frequently sang the words of the popular tune of the day:

> To the West, to the West, to the land of the free,
> Where the mighty Missouri rolls down to the sea;
> Where a man is a man even though he must toil
> And the poorest may gather the fruits of the soil.

As soon as the family boarded the former whaling ship, the *Wiscasset*, which set sail from the Firth of Forth on May 17, 1848, he eagerly explored every nook and cranny and introduced himself to the crew and passengers. He was a good sailor, and he was brimming over with energy and ebullient spirits; wisely, the captain kept him out of mischief by making him a cabin boy for the duration of the voyage.

Finally, after fifty days at sea, the *Wiscasset* dropped anchor in New York Harbor. But the Carnegies' odyssey was far from over. It took them three weeks to travel by barge on the Erie Canal to the town of Allegheny, which is now a part of Pittsburgh, Pennsylvania. Margaret's sisters arranged for them to live rent-free for the time being in two back-alley rooms of a squalid boarding house. William got a job in a cotton mill, but, disgusted with the work, he quit after a few months, rented a primitive loom, and began hawking his humble wares door to door. Margaret sold groceries in a general store and bound shoes for a cobbler. And twelve-year-old Andrew gave up school to work as a bobbin boy in a cotton mill. He worked a twelve-hour shift, from 6:00 A.M. to 6:00 P.M., for $1.20 a week. Many years afterward, he wrote an article called, "How I Served My Apprenticeship," which appeared in the popular magazine, *Youth's Companion:*

> I cannot tell you how proud I was when I received my first week's own earnings. One dollar and twenty cents made by myself and given to me because I had been of some use in the world! No longer entirely dependent on my parents, but at last admitted to the family partnership as a contributing member and able to help them! I think this makes a man out of a boy sooner than almost anything else, and a real man, too, if there be any germ of true manhood in him. It is everything to feel that you are useful.
>
> I have had to deal with great sums. Many millions of dollars have since passed through my hands. But the genuine satisfaction I had from that one dollar and twenty cents outweighs any subsequent pleasure in money-getting. It was the direct reward of honest, manual labor; it represented a week of very hard work—so hard that, but for the aim end which sanctified it, slavery might not be too strong a term to describe it.

It was indeed hard work for a boy. He then volunteered for the even more difficult job of tending a steam boiler because it paid two dollars a week. He worked day after day all alone in a dark room filled with intense heat and noise. On his own initiative, he took night classes to learn double-entry bookkeeping, and he soon graduated to helping with his employer's accounting and working in the vat room, where he had to dip bobbins in great cauldrons of oil, which was nauseating work because of the smell.

Then at fourteen, he was offered the chance to become a messenger boy in the telegraph business. In his own words, it was like being "carried from darkness to light." Though being a messenger boy was a challenge for one who barely knew his way around the city, Andrew did not let it stop him. In his off-hours, he roamed around Pittsburgh memorizing the names of streets and businesses. He also practiced on the telegraph machines early in the morning before the operators arrived. At fifteen, he was promoted to telegraph operator, and before long he was taking messages by ear. All but a handful of operators in the nation had to record messages on paper before they could decipher them. Andrew's feat made him a minor celebrity in the city. But most important of all, he was now earning twenty-five dollars a month. He had fulfilled his boyhood vow of rescuing his family from poverty. And the Carnegies could at last afford to move into a house of their own. The mortgage would take years to pay off, however, so everyone (except young Tom, who was still in school) toiled just as hard as before. Andrew even took on a second job, preparing telegraph dispatches for newspaper reporters for one dollar a week.

IN 1853, HE JOINED the Pennsylvania Railroad as a telegraph operator. Shortly after he was hired, a major accident occurred that stopped traffic on the northbound, southbound, and westbound lines. Superintendent Scott was late, and no one knew when he would arrive. So, the eighteen-year-old Andrew took charge, issuing orders in his boss's name that quickly had the trains up and running again. When Scott arrived and ascertained what had happened, he said nothing at all. But he was never late again, and he confided to at least one associate that he'd seldom seen anyone as brave or resourceful as that "little white-haired Scotch devil." Later, he made Andrew his assistant.

It was a promotion that William Carnegie did not live to see. He died in 1855 at age fifty-one, broken in spirit and body. Andrew was devastated. He loved his father dearly, and referred to him as "one of the most lovable of men...not much of a man of the world, but a man all over for heaven." When he was transferred to Altoona, Pennsylvania, Andrew insisted that Margaret and Tom move with him. He could not bear to part from the two remaining members of his family.

In 1856, he ghostwrote a manual on the railroad telegraph system. In the same year, Superintendent Scott came to him and asked if he had five hundred dollars to invest; a man who owned ten shares of stock in the Adams Express Company had died and the shares were up for private sale. When he came to her for advice, his mother suggested mortgaging the house, and he readily agreed. It was a gamble, but it paid off; the Carnegies' first monthly dividend check was for the handsome sum of five dollars. "Here was something new to all of us," Andrew said, "for none of us had ever received anything but from toil. A return from capital was something strange and new." In 1859, he earned yet another promotion; when his boss was appointed as a vice president of the railroad, he took over as superintendent of the entire western division. Once again, the Carnegies packed up their belongings and headed back to Pittsburgh.

In his new role, Andrew was to make many improvements in efficiency and organization. He spent as much time observing what was going on in the railyards as what was going on in the offices.[4] He was like a dynamo, always stirring things up, always on the move, and always looking for ways to make things better. He hired the first female telegraph operators in the country. He also helped introduce the first railway sleeping cars. And while he worked tirelessly to make the western division a success, he also spared the time to make small investments in manufactures and in the fledgling petroleum industry that would net big gains in the years to come.

---

4   Spending so much time in the railyards presented a problem; the men were always shoving Andrew out of the way or running him off because they thought he was a trespassing youth. He decided to grow a beard in order to appear older, but, at age twenty-four, he still didn't look much like a railroad boss.

IN THE SPRING OF 1861, when civil war seemed inevitable, Andrew accepted an invitation from the War Department to come to Washington, D.C., and help organize a military telegraph service. He was eager to serve the Union cause for, since coming to America, he had been active in the abolitionist movement. He believed that ending slavery was not enough; blacks had to be given voting rights and property rights. He was forced to give up several personal friendships and he risked his new, elevated status in Pittsburgh social circles because of his views, but he didn't back down. And shortly after the fall of Fort Sumter in April, he had the opportunity to act upon them. Maryland secessionists cut the telegraph lines and destroyed the bridges around Washington. The capital was in desperate straits, with no communications or troops. Andrew rounded up a crew and repaired the bridge at a main junction. He then commandeered a train to carry a relief force into the city. Thousands of citizens, including President Abraham Lincoln, turned out to cheer the rescuers. At the Battle of Bull Run in July, his talent for organization and decisiveness was again critical. He set up an elaborate courier system to carry military dispatches and supervised the loading of the wounded on trains. Risking capture by the Confederates, he remained in the field until nightfall, when the last train steamed back to Alexandria.

Andrew was like a dynamo, always stirring things up, always on the move, and always looking for ways to make things better.

As assistant in charge of railroads and telegraph service for the entire northern army, Andrew saw the early progress of the war from a unique vantage point. His office in the War Department building "was the center for all the incoming dispatches from the field. President Lincoln was a frequent visitor, half-sitting, half-leaning against Carnegie's desk, waiting for a reply to some dispatch, and all the while talking to whoever had the time to listen." Undoubtedly, he found this exciting, but he was more impressed by the horrors of war, which he had seen firsthand, and by the appalling inefficiency of the military. In September, he was glad to go back to Pittsburgh, where he was needed to keep open the western division of the Pennsylvania Railroad. He threw himself into recruiting telegraph operators and linemen, repairing destroyed routes, establishing military depots, and building more sidings and railyards to accommodate the tremendous increase in freight.

In the summer of 1862, suffering from exhaustion and the aftereffects of a severe case of sunstroke, he applied for a three-month leave of absence. It was Andrew's first vacation since he had begun to work in the cotton mills as a bobbin boy fourteen years earlier. He and his mother decided to make a pilgrimage back to Scotland. Although he was overjoyed to see Dunfermline and all his aunts and uncles and cousins again, he caught pneumonia and was deathly ill for weeks. Finally, he recovered, and he and Margaret sailed home. They traveled first class on the two-week voyage. Clearly, much had changed since they had come over on the *Wiscasset* in 1848.

EVEN THOUGH HE WAS now a rich man, Andrew immediately went back to work. He did not care that the railroad was taking up huge amounts of his time and energy; he refused to resign until the war was over.[5] In 1864, he took another brief leave and went on a walking tour of Europe. He left his brother Tom in charge of his business ventures, which were quite diverse by this time. He was never so caught up in business that he could not occasionally take time off to do other things that he considered important. He reflected, "In this world we must learn not to lay up our treasures, but to enjoy them day by day as we travel the path we never return to."

---

5   In 1863, for example, Andrew made a salary of $2,400 from the railroad and $47,000 from his investments.

He also studied with tutors to make up for the lack of a formal education. Although he was desirous of gaining some social polish, he was not out to ingratiate himself with the members of high society but to slake his genuine thirst for knowledge. He justified his effort by remarking, "It has been said that you can educate a man too much. You might as well tell me you could have a man too sober." He even organized a discussion club to debate political, economic, and social issues. He loved to meet people whose ideas he found interesting. Over the years, he gained such friends and acquaintances as Mark Twain, Ralph Waldo Emerson, Julia Ward Howe, Matthew Arnold, Bronson Alcott, Herbert Spencer, and Booker T. Washington, as well as Britain's Prime Minister William Gladstone and every president of the United States from Abraham Lincoln to Woodrow Wilson. What is important to note is that Andrew "never kowtowed to anyone, however important." Even as an ambitious youth, he refused to curry favor or meet anyone except "on a frank and equal basis."

When the war was over, he organized the Freedom Iron and Steel Company and the Keystone Bridgeworks to build some of the world's first iron railroad bridges. These were a vast technological improvement because they could withstand flood and fire. Andrew loved building bridges. He saw them as

> great edifices, the best in American architectural design, engineering skill, and iron manufacturing—mighty monuments that would endure for generations as testimonials to the practical application of technical genius. The great bridges over the Ohio, Mississippi, and Missouri not only fulfilled the urgent practical need of carrying traffic across the continent, but they were aesthetically and philosophically satisfying as well. There was a beauty of design, given its reality in great iron beams, cables, and stone pylons. There was the symbolism of the Union, so meaningful to a nation that had been but recently torn apart by civil war. All of this Carnegie found deeply moving and gratifying.

Freedom and Keystone were successes because Andrew was a superb salesman, but it was his insistence on superior quality that really paid off. When a project to build a bridge in Susquehanna was in trouble, he wrote to the supervisor in charge:

> I agree with you that it is vital to the interest of our Keystone Bridge Co., that we should get this contract to keep our men together. It is out of the question to expect profit out of it. However this may be, we must maintain our policy: put nothing but the best triple rolled iron in our structures, and let the concerns like Edgemoor, which buys the cheapest and meanest stuff in the merchant market, run their course.
>
> We cannot afford to have an accident to one of our bridges.... [I]f we stand firm on quality, we must win.

Andrew also built the iron and steel exhibition hall—the first of its kind—for the Centennial Exhibition of 1876 and the skeleton of the first steel-frame office building. But his love of building tangible things soon led him into the world of high finance, where intangibles were the name of the game. To raise capital for his own expanding enterprises as well as for the railroads that hired him to serve as an agent, he traveled to Europe in 1869 to sell bonds, i.e., interest-bearing certificates promising to pay the bearer guaranteed sums on specific dates. Over four years, he sold an incredible $30 million in bonds. As usual, he knew next to nothing about the business when he first began, but he quickly mastered even the most arcane details. The self-educated Scotsman became well known as a powerful financier whose knowledge rivaled the heads of the great banking houses of the world. His particular strength was that he was a cool and patient negotiator. He did not close a deal unless he was satisfied with the terms and with all parties' ability to deliver on their promises. His reputation for honesty and integrity was also unquestioned; Andrew's word was quite literally his bond.

IN 1873, DESPITE A SEVERE BANKING CRISIS that plunged the nation into depression, he started construction on a state-of-the-art steel plant called the Edgar Thomson Steel Works. He paid no attention to the doomsayers who predicted his downfall; he knew that he could actually benefit from the financial downturn. With so many businesses idle, he could get a bargain on everything from raw materials and labor to equipment and freight charges. And because most steel works were cutting back dramatically on production, his company's products would fill a void in the market. The Age of Steel was taking over from the Age of Iron, and Andrew wanted to be in the forefront. By 1887, all his steel mills, which would eventually be united as the Carnegie Steel Company, were earning $3.5 million a year. By 1900, they were earning $40 million and producing one quarter of all the steel in the nation.[6]

What was Andrew's secret? According to the conventional wisdom, he was nothing but a "robber baron." This term, which has become synonymous with another epithet, "greedy capitalist," refers to medieval knights who forced travelers to pay outrageous tolls to cross their lands. The principal evidence critics like to present is his alleged hypocrisy in regard to labor unions. In 1886 millions of Americans reacted with horror to the violence that erupted during the McCormick Harvester Works strike in Chicago. A demonstration in Haymarket Square turned into a riot when a bomb was thrown at the police. Seven officers and four workers were killed. Eight alleged anarchists were later arrested, and four were executed. A short time later, in two widely read magazine articles, Andrew stunned the nation by taking up the cause, not of the owners, but of the strikers. Capital is not "the natural enemy of labor," he declared, but it is only

---

6 To give you another idea of how quickly Andrew's empire grew: In 1885, Great Britain was the world's leading steel producer; by 1899, the Carnegie Steel Company was producing 695,000 tons more steel than all the companies in Britain combined.

natural that each group looks to its own interests. Workers, therefore, are entitled to form unions. He even expressed sympathy for some strikers who had committed illegal acts because they were driven to desperation.

But then Andrew's ideals were put to the test. In 1892, while he was vacationing in Scotland, workers at the Carnegie Steel Company's Homestead Steel Works near Pittsburgh went on strike. His partner Henry Frick deliberately provoked the walkout, hoping to destroy the union. As soon as the last worker departed from the grounds, he put up barbed wire and hired armed Pinkerton guards. There was a bloody confrontation in which ten men were killed and sixty were wounded. Eventually the strike was called off, and the union admitted defeat. The press attacked Andrew without mercy. He was accused of conspiring with Frick and leaving the country to avoid being implicated. An editorial in the *St. Louis Post-Dispatch* summed up how public opinion had turned against him: "Three months ago Andrew Carnegie was a man to be envied. Today he is an object of mingled pity and contempt."

But the real record casts doubt on the charges against Andrew. For one thing, he was not a hypocrite on the subject of unions. As his principal biographer pointed out, he favored unions formed by the workers within individual companies in response to specific grievances, not national unions that had a bigger agenda, which was wresting control of companies away from the owners. About eight hundred of the nearly four thousand men who worked at Homestead belonged to the Amalgamated Association of Iron and Steel Workers (AAISW), a "fiercely elitist" organization that allowed only skilled employees in certain divisions to join its ranks. Members of the union received significantly higher wages than nonunion workers, and when Carnegie Steel spent millions of dollars to put in new furnaces and other equipment that increased production, they saw a 60 percent increase in what they earned for doing the same amount of work. Andrew wanted to split the difference after the old contract expired and pay them only 30 percent more, but the union balked. In addition to keeping the entire 60 percent, the AAISW demanded power over hiring and firing policies; the replacement of many nonunion workers with hand-picked union substitutes brought over from Europe; input about technical aspects of the steelmaking process; and a final say in setting the prices that would be charged for finished products.

Knowing of these demands, Andrew correctly perceived that the AAISW was a threat to nonunion workers and to his own management of the company. Just before he left for Scotland, he prepared an open letter to all employees that Frick was instructed to post (but never did) outlining his intention to make Homestead a nonunion plant after the expiration of the current contract. He concluded, "This action is not taken in any spirit of hostility to labor organizations, but every man will see that the firm cannot run Union and Non-Union. It must be one or the other." He knew that his decision might result in a strike; he had weathered several before. But he had always managed to avert violence by stating his position openly and forthrightly, by making reasonable compromises at the bargaining table, and, most important of all, by refusing to hire strikebreakers. On several occasions he had closed his plants for months on end, at a cost of millions of dollars, because he wanted the jobs to be there for his men when they returned. "Thou shalt not take thy neighbor's job," was his Golden Rule. But Henry Frick had no such scruples, and he hired "scabs." It was these replacement workers marching into the Homestead plant under armed guard that caused the fighting. Upon hearing about the incident, Andrew was furious with Frick for disobeying his orders. His first impulse was to come home at once and sort things out, but the board of directors convinced him that it was better to remain out of the picture entirely. When he finally

Even though he was now a rich man, Andrew immediately went back to work. He refused to resign until the war was over.

realized that this only made him look responsible for the whole affair, it was too late to do anything.

He worked his men hard, and he wasn't above trying to scrimp on labor costs, but, by the standards of the day, Andrew was regarded as a progressive employer. He experimented, for example, with three eight-hour shifts at one of his steel plants in the 1880s. This was unheard of in an industry where the twelve-hour shift was the norm. He tried to get other firms to adopt the same reform. Only when the competition refused to go along, and when it became clear that the plant was losing as much as $500,000 a year, did he reluctantly revert to the old system. The men went on strike to protest. He closed the plant and suffered greater losses even though he could have easily hired replacements. After four months, the strikers relented and asked to return to work. He offered them a choice: continuance of the eight-hour day at less pay or a return to the twelve-hour day under a new profit-sharing plan that would raise every worker's base salary according to a sliding scale based on the market price of steel. Not surprisingly, the strikers voted to return to the twelve-hour schedule.

When he worked for the railroad, Andrew "would go out in all kinds of weather, work for twenty-four hours without a rest, and expect his men to do the same." When he became the head of the Carnegie Steel Company, he never recruited "his leaders on the basis of wealth or family standing. He used a merit system; he wanted people who could make the best steel possible at the lowest price." And when he finally sold out to U.S. Steel, he gave $5 million outright to his employees for a pension and benefit fund. Are these the actions of a robber baron? Hardly. He had serious faults to be sure, but more than anything else, Andrew was a creator. He created new products, new jobs, and new wealth. He created modernization of industry, financial institutions, and credit. He created competition. He even created a new breed of entrepreneur, one who knew "the whole market, present and future, being ever alert to the potentialities of change." And in doing all this, he took enormous risks. Many careers, fortunes, and reputations were lost as a result of a single shift on the stock market, a change in the weather, the collapse of a bank, a contract dispute, a financial panic, a lawsuit, or the arbitrary dictates of a lone government official. He himself lost millions of dollars over the years, but he never allowed himself to become complacent or timid.

Although he often claimed, "pioneering don't pay," Andrew was also an innovator. It was at the Carnegie Steel Company, for example, that a new mixer was invented (keeping pig iron molten before it was fed into the furnace to be made into steel) and that automatic feeding machines (to feed raw materials into the furnaces, move cast steel, and load and unload boxcars) were developed. The result was a huge savings in terms of time and money, a huge increase in production, and a huge decrease in consumer prices. Why did Andrew place so much emphasis on innovation? In part, it was because he had witnessed the tragic results of

> Andrew did not close a deal unless he was satisfied with the terms and with all parties' ability to deliver on their promises. His reputation for honesty and integrity was also unquestioned; Andrew's word was quite literally his bond.

his father's unwillingness to adapt to change. But he was also committed to trying new ways of doing things because he was a passionate cost-cutter. His favorite motto was, "Watch the costs, and the profits will take care of themselves." Said one source, "At the heart of Carnegie's system were bonuses and partnerships for those who excelled. Strong incentives were given employees who could figure out how to save on iron ore, coke, and limestone; or how to produce a harder, cheaper steel; or how to capture new markets for steel." He paid one of his mill superintendents who had come up through the ranks and who had a knack for coming up with new inventions twenty-five thousand dollars a year—the same salary paid to the president of the United States. Andrew also urged his employees to find new uses for waste products. Thus, when other steel companies were throwing away "scale," the steel shavings that were left over after the rolling process, Carnegie Steel was melting it down to make new steel rails; the company even sent men to offer to cart it away from other plants for a fee. And it used "flue cinder," a by-product from the blast furnaces that was universally regarded as worthless, as a highly concentrated and efficient fuel. The company was also the first to boast a full-time chemist and research department dedicated to developing methods of recycling and quality control. Furthermore, when the railroad boom and the sale of steel rails reached their peak, Andrew and Carnegie Steel were ahead of the pack in discovering new markets for construction beams, ship plating, buggy springs, stovepipes, and plows.

But none of the efforts to minimize costs and maximize profits came at the expense of quality. Andrew always maintained, "I have never known a concern to make a decided success that did not do good, honest work, and even in these days of the fiercest competition, when everything would seem to be a matter of price, there lies still at the root of great business success the very much more important factor of quality."

January 1901

Andrew pulled out the letter from the top drawer of his desk and read it slowly, even though he had practically memorized its contents over the years. He had written it as a memorandum to himself when he was thirty-three and making all of fifty thousand a year. My, but that seemed like a lot of money back then! The crucial passage read:

Man must have an idol—the amassing of wealth is one of the worst species of idolatry—no idol more debasing than the worship of money. Whatever I engage in, I must push inordinately; therefore I should be careful to choose that life which will be most elevating in its character.

How true those words were then and now. He was sixty-five years old, and one of the richest men in the world. So what was he to do next? He didn't fancy the idea of retirement, but he knew that he must stop accumulating and begin the infinitely more serious task of distributing his wealth. He wished his mother Margaret and his brother Tom were present to help him. But they had died within a few weeks of each other back in 1886. His only comfort now was his dear, sweet Louise, whom he had married in 1887 after a long courtship, and their precious daughter, Margaret, who was born a decade later. For far too long, he had let his business interests take center stage. Now it was time to devote himself to his family and to "giving" instead of "getting." It was true that he had donated to charity all his life, but now he wanted to make a career of it, and he brought to this new enterprise all the driving determination and energy that had led to his meteoric rise in the steel industry.

He called the visitor who had been waiting in the front parlor, Carnegie Steel President Charles Schwab, into his study.

"So, Charlie, as I understand it from our conversation of yesterday afternoon, our old friend on Wall Street, J.P. Morgan, has put together a wee little concern by the name of U.S. Steel for the express purpose of buying our company?"

"That's not exactly how I would describe it. He's put together a super-corporation consisting of National Steel, American Steel & Wire, and American Tin Plate. Once Carnegie Steel is added to this list, he will have the world's first billion-dollar business."

Andrew mused, "Well, the wily old fox is welcome to it, and I wish him good fortune. As for me, I have more important things to occupy my time." He picked up a blunt pencil stub and wrote on a small scrap of paper:

*Capitalization of the Carnegie Company:
$160,000,000 bonds to be exchanged
at par for bonds in new company
$160,000,000*

*$160,000,000 stock to be exchanged
at a rate of $1,000 share of stock
in Carnegie Company exchanged
for $1,500 share of stock in new company
$240,000,000*

*Profit of past year and estimated
profit for coming year
$80,000,000*

*Total price for Carnegie Company and
all its holdings
$480,000,000*

And then he said, "Please take this to Mr. Morgan if you will be so kind, and inquire if my terms are agreeable to the gentleman."

Schwab looked down at the scrap that had been thrust into his hand. The biggest sale in American history was about to be consummated with all the formality of an errand boy's taking a shopping list to the corner grocery store.[7] "Why not demand some of this in stock instead of bonds? If you are the majority stockholder, you will still be able to vote on all the company's important business decisions. And, while you're at it, why don't you have our lawyers draw up a more iron-clad contract?"

"No, I won't play the role of Banquo's ghost—the spectre at the feast, that is. I am retiring from business.

---

[7] This sentence is a paraphrase of Joseph Frazier Wall's.

Besides, bonds are more easy to transfer to other parties, which is what I have in mind. As for a contract, no doubt J.P. will insist on drawing one up later on. But I think he will be more than willing to sign this agreement, and he will honor it as binding."

A few hours later, Schwab returned to Andrew's residence on fashionable 51st Street in New York. Sheepishly, he said, "You were right, Andy. All Morgan said was, 'I accept this price,' and he signed your note like it was any ordinary receipt." He plopped down on a chair and rubbed his glistening forehead with a handkerchief. "I must say, in all my years in business, I have never seen anything to compare with the two of you—you're the last of a dying breed."

"It's a go, then," Andrew replied. Under his breath, he added, "One dream dies, so another may begin. At least I hope it may." He was not by nature a secretive man, but he would not care for Schwab to know how much it cost him to quit the business he had built from the ground up. It was the hardest thing he had ever done in a life in which hard decisions had become a routine affair.

After Schwab departed, he went upstairs to the nursery where Louise was sitting on the couch reading a book of fairy tales to four-year-old Margaret. He settled in comfortably next to them and whispered in his wife's ear, "It's done, my dear."

She stopped reading for a minute. "It's about time," she said with mock severity. Then, she went back to recounting the tale of "The Princess and the Pea," mimicking all the character's voices to Margaret's delight.

Andrew watched her tenderly. As New York's most eligible bachelor, he could have chosen a grand beauty who would outshine all the other society hostesses. But Louise, who was shy and quietly attractive, "had a way with her." She was the kindest, gentlest person he had ever met, and the smile that was slowly spreading across her features as she

pretended to ignore his scrutiny went straight to his heart.
No blast furnace on earth could produce such warmth. He
knew then that everything was going to be all right.

WHEN THE FORMAL CONTRACT (which the famous financier
J.P. Morgan did insist upon) was signed in February of 1901 and
the Carnegie Steel Company was sold, Andrew's share was worth
over $225 million. Even before the sale was final, he knew what
he would do with this enormous windfall. In 1889, he had written an essay called "The Gospel of Wealth." In it, he proposed
that successful businessmen are trustees of their wealth with a
God-given responsibility to use it to help others, first in their own
communities where they can immediately see what is wanted,
and then in the larger world.[8] This essay had a tremendous influence on American society. Never before had a businessman
reached millions of people with his message, and what a message
it was! Andrew claimed to settle once and for all the old debate
over what to do about "economic injustice" and the "unequal
distribution" of wealth: The wealthy should volunteer to give
their wealth away. Why? He answered this question by quoting
Jesus, "It is easier for a camel to enter the eye of a needle than for
a rich man to enter the kingdom of heaven," and by adding that
the rich man who gives away his wealth while leading a virtuous

---

8   As I indicated earlier, there are scholars, mainly on the Left, who doubt that
Andrew's message was sincere. Time and time again, they have caricatured
him as a money-grubbing robber baron who ruthlessly pursued wealth and
then gave most of it to charity in order to ease his guilty conscience and "buy
posterity." Why have they treated one of the nation's greatest businessmen as
if he were a villain instead of a hero? I would argue that it is because they
automatically associate capitalism with greed and materialism. They do not
understand that capitalism is the most moral of all economic systems because
it leaves men free to make their own decisions and because it makes serving
others (consumers) the primary interest of the entrepreneur. Yes, it is true that
many men (scholars as well as businessmen) are greedy and materialistic, but
they would be so under any system.

life will find that his riches "will not be a bar to heaven." He even went so far as to endorse an inheritance tax, believing that "the man who dies rich dies disgraced."[9]

But it was not enough for Andrew to say that the wealthy must distribute their wealth. He had very specific ideas about how it must be distributed. He did not endorse bequeathing more than a reasonable sum to one's heirs, for he believed that great inherited wealth is a burden to those who have not earned it and a catalyst for the moral and cultural breakdown of society. "To be born to honest poverty and compelled to labor and strive for a livelihood in youth is the best of all schools for developing latent qualities, strengthening character, and making useful men," he said. He also pointed out, "As a rule there is more genuine satisfaction, a truer life, and more obtained from life in the humble cottages of the poor than in the palaces of the rich." Of course, he was not referring to grinding poverty but to humble circumstances that demand industriousness, prudence, foresight, and thriftiness from an early age.

Andrew further stipulated that wealth must be distributed during the earner's lifetime. This mode of philanthropy would be far less likely to do harm, he argued. He was deeply concerned about this since, in his opinion, "of every thousand dollars spent in so-called charity today, it is probable that nine hundred and fifty dollars is unwisely spent—so spent, indeed, as to produce the very evils which it hopes to mitigate or cure." In the same vein, he wrote, "A man may accumulate great wealth in a democracy, but he has a responsibility to return that wealth in a way that will not destroy society's own responsibility to preserve individual initiative." In other words, he was aware, as few people ever have been, that indiscriminate charity can be dangerous. When criticized for his uncompromising stance on this issue, he referred to a passage

---

[9]   Notably, however, he opposed the income tax and Henry George's popular proposal to tax landowners.

from the ancient Greek philosopher Plutarch's *Morals* in which a beggar asks a wealthy passerby for alms and the passerby replies, "Well, should I give thee anything, thou wilt be the greater beggar, for he that first gave thee money made thee idle, and is the cause of this base and dishonorable way of living."

He enumerated what projects were most worthy of support: employee pensions, libraries, hospitals, universities, museums, churches, parks, public baths, shelters for the poor, and foundations dedicated to promoting education, peace, and cultural renewal. His own gifts underwrote countless such projects, the most famous being Carnegie Hall (1892), the Carnegie Institution (1902), the Carnegie Hero Fund Commission (1904), the Carnegie Foundation for the Advancement of Teaching (1905), and the Carnegie Endowment for International Peace (1910). He also sent children to Paris to be treated by Louis Pasteur for rabies, supported associations for the blind because of his admiration for Helen Keller, and gave research grants to such pioneering scientists as France's Polish-born radiation expert, Marie Curie, and Alabama's ex-slave and agriculturist, George Washington Carver. Unquestionably, his most popular gift was the establishment of 2,811 libraries. Today, the free library seems "as much a part of America as the schoolhouse or the church," but it was practically nonexistent in the early twentieth century. Andrew thought of free libraries as the people's universities, and he gave personal testimony to support this idea:

> When I was a working boy in Pittsburgh, Colonel Anderson of Allegheny—a name I can never speak without feelings of devotional gratitude—opened his little library of four hundred books to boys. Every Saturday afternoon he was in attendance in his house to exchange books. No one but he who has felt it can ever know the intense longing with which the arrival of Saturday was awaited, that a new book might be had.

Ironically, his first attempt to emulate Colonel Anderson was a failure. The Pittsburgh City Council spurned his proposed gift of two hundred and fifty thousand dollars for a public library building because it would have had to purchase the books. Andrew always insisted that charity had to be a partnership— those on the receiving end must make a commitment to help themselves; they could not merely expect handouts. Eventually, the council changed its position and accepted one million dollars for a library and even more for an art museum and a concert hall.

Early on, Andrew learned that giving away money was not the simple affair he assumed it would be. After receiving thousands of "begging letters," he was moved to remark, "Pity the poor millionaire, for the way of the philanthropist is hard." He had to procure secretaries whose sole function was to open the mail and advisors to help him decide which causes and individuals to support. But he never retreated from the process; he handled many cases personally, displaying "extraordinary patience and sensitivity." Quite a few of his gifts were anonymous, too. Andrew was "not trying to buy his way into Heaven"; he was following the charge of John Wesley, founder of Methodism: "Gain all you can; save all you can; and then give all you can to do good to all men." And how faithfully did he live up to this charge? You be the judge: He gave away 90 percent of his wealth—*over three hundred and fifty million dollars.*

But no biography of Andrew Carnegie can be complete if it tells only the story of his life as a struggling rags-to-riches hero or business tycoon or philanthropist. He was also a patriot who loved America with a passion that knew no bounds. He prized republican democracy and disdained the old European aristocratic system. In his 1886 book, *Triumphant Democracy,* he wrote: "The unity of the American people is further powerfully promoted by the foundation upon which the political structure rests, the equality of the citizen. There is not one shred of privilege to be met with anywhere in all the laws." He wrote this book because he wanted to impress upon his fellow Americans all that their country had achieved and could achieve. But he also wanted to destroy certain misconceptions Europeans had about the American character and the genius of the American system. For instance, he went to great pains to rebut the oft-repeated charge that such an egalitarian nation could not produce or sustain high culture:

Who knows or cares who Michelangelo's father was or what was Beethoven's birth, or whether Raphael was an aristocrat, or Wagner the son of a poor actuary of police? Just imagine a monarchy in art—a hereditary painter, for instance, or a sculptor who was only his father's son, or a musician, because born in the profession!...

This curious writer, who would have monarchy allied with art, built his theory on the exploded idea that only monarchs and the aristocracy, which flutters around the courts, could or would patronize the beautiful. That theory is unfortunate, in view of the fact that the best patrons of art are the Americans.

He rarely resorted to humor, but he could not resist repeating a joke in his observations in the same book about the decadence of Great Britain's ruling class:

When the fair young American asked the latest lordling who did her country the honor to visit it, how the aristocratic leisure classes spent their time, he replied: "Oh, they go from one house to another, don't you know, and enjoy themselves, you know. They never do any work, you know." "Oh," she replied, "we have such people too—tramps."

Triumphant Democracy created a literary sensation in the United States and abroad. It sold tens of thousands of copies and went into numerous reprintings. Andrew was prompted by its reception to go on the lecture circuit. At one 1887 public address in Scotland called "Home Rule in America," he gave a marvelously succinct and accurate description of how the system of republican government works. He also delivered this wry observation about the presidency:

> We make our king every four years and we pay him a tremendous salary. I suppose all you people would grudge it for a crowned head. We pay him ten thousand pounds per annum, and we have nothing to do with his brothers and his sisters, and his cousins and his aunts. And at the end of four years, if we do not like him, we put him down and elect another one.

In addition, Andrew told his audience that American democracy went hand in hand with a free market economy. Although he admired the humane goals of socialism and indeed shared them, he knew socialism could not work in practice. He was a devout believer in Adam Smith, not Karl Marx, and he linked the rise of civilization directly to the rise of capitalism.[10] Before the introduction of the factory system, wages were low, unemployment was high, and the "mode of manufacture was crude articles at high prices." Now, he said, the reverse was true, and he expounded on this theme:

> ...civilization took its start from the day when the capable, industrial workman said to his incompetent and lazy fellow, "If thou dost not sow, thou shalt not reap," and thus ended primitive Communism by separating the drones from the bees. One who studies this subject will soon be brought face to face with the conclusion that upon the sacredness of property civilization depends—the right

---

10 Adam Smith was a Scottish moral philosopher who wrote *The Wealth of Nations* (1776). Today, this book remains the most important and profound study of human action in the marketplace ever written. German philosopher Karl Marx's monument to socialism, *Das Capital* (1867), on the other hand, has been thoroughly discredited.

of the laborer to his hundred dollars in the savings-bank, and equally the legal right of the millionaire to his millions. Every man must be allowed "to sit under his own vine and fig-tree, with none to make afraid," if human society is to advance, or even to remain so far advanced as it is.

As a consequence, he concluded:

> The poor enjoy what the rich could not before afford. What were the luxuries have become the necessities of life. The laborer now has more comforts than the farmer had a few generations ago. The farmer has more luxuries than the landlord had, and is more richly clad and better housed. The landlord has books and pictures rarer and appointments more artistic than the king could then obtain.

He also disputed the notion that the rich got rich by exploiting the poor. On the issue of property, he noted that while in 1850 there were fewer than a million and a half farmers who owned their farms, in 1880 over four million had become landowners. As for "growing poverty," he reported that one out of every five men, women, and children in New England and the Middle States had savings accounts and that the 1880 census listed fewer than ninety thousand paupers in a population of fifty million. (Most of these were aged or recent immigrants.) But Andrew did not preach that capitalism was a utopian system, that human nature and therefore human institutions could be free of flaws, that there are no limits to progress, or that every wrong can be righted. He was deeply conscious that there was a price for all the "salutary changes" wrought by capitalism, and he admitted as much:

> We assemble thousands of operatives in the factory, and in the mine, of whom the employer can know little or nothing, and to whom he is little better than a myth. All intercourse between them

is at an end. Rigid castes are formed, and, as usual, mutual ignorance breeds distrust.

The answer to these problems lay in the principles of philanthropic
charity laid out in "The Gospel of Wealth" and in its corollary:
spiritual charity. Andrew's parents were "Nonconformists" who
rejected the stern doctrines of Scottish Calvinism, but they taught
him to appreciate the basic tenets of Christianity and the value of
leading a moral life. Unlike many of his peers, he studied the
Scriptures, lived frugally, practiced individual acts of mercy, and
avoided gambling, excessive drinking, and womanizing. The deca-
dent habits of the privileged classes, or what we today call the
"lifestyles of the rich and famous," held no temptation for him.
Much has been made of Andrew's public declaration that he had
found a new theology in the secular Darwinian and Spencerian
concepts of the "survival of the fittest," but he was really only
endorsing the optimistic generalization that "all is well since all
grows better." He explained his attitude by stating that man

> has implanted within him the instinct which compels him to turn
> his face to the sun and slowly move upward toward that which is
> better, rejecting in his progress after test, all that injures or debases,
> the call upon us by our Socialist friends to exchange the individu-
> alistic civilized present which we have reached after many hundreds
> of thousands of years of progress, for the system of communism of
> the savage past is indeed startling.

He also said on numerous occasions that "the best worship of
God is serving man," and he urged wealthy businessmen to live
in imitation of "the spirit of Christ" by "laboring for the good of
our fellows, which was the essence of his life and teaching...." It
was precisely such spiritual beliefs that led Andrew to be an out-
spoken pacifist. Although he acknowledged the need for a strong
army and navy, he hated war. He had tasted its bitter fruits from

1861 to 1865, and he believed the United States should never again take up arms except in its own defense. He opposed the Spanish–American War, and relented only when his friends convinced him that helping Cuba win its freedom from Spain was a just cause. But when the terms of peace in 1898 allowed the United States to annex the Philippines, he rounded condemned American imperialism. As with his crusade against slavery, he did not care if his strong convictions made him unpopular or hurt his reputation. He publicly challenged the McKinley administration's justification that it was part of the "white man's burden" to take over the administration of foreign lands by quoting President Lincoln: "When the white man governs himself, that is self-government; but when he governs himself and also governs another man, that is more than self-government, that is despotism."

Obviously, Andrew did not fit the stereotype of the American businessman in the so-called "Gilded Age." Another trait that revealed his many-faceted character was his love for the intellectual life. His favorite books were by Marcus Aurelius, Milton, Shakespeare, Goethe, Thomas Carlyle, Matthew Arnold, Alfred Tennyson, and Robert Burns. He wrote nearly sixty essays of his own for some of the most prestigious literary magazines in the United States and Great Britain, two travel books, *Round the World* (1878) and *An American Four-in-Hand in Britain* (1883), and five books on politics, economics, history, and philanthropy: *Triumphant Democracy* (1886), *The Gospel of Wealth and Other Essays* (1900), *The Empire of Business* (1902), *James Watt* (1905), and *Problems of Today* (1908). His autobiography, which he began in 1891, was published posthumously in 1920. "Even as a teen," stated a biographer, Andrew "was a writer, and writing was his great outlet." His wrote his first letter to a newspaper in 1853; by the time he was in his eighties he had seen nearly two hundred printed. He believed that it was not only a right but a responsibility for citizens to make their voices heard: "If any man wants *bona fide* substantial power and influence in this world, he must handle the pen. That's flat. Truly it is a nobler weapon than the sword, and a much nobler one than the tongue, both of which have nearly had their day."

Andrew spent his last years in a tireless—and often fruitless—crusade to establish international peace. Just two weeks before his eighty-third birthday, the armistice was signed that ended the terrible carnage of World War I. It was the happiest event in his life in many years, and the capstone was his beloved daughter Margaret's marriage to a young American ensign shortly afterward. He died at his Shadowbrook estate in Massachusetts on August 11, 1919. He accomplished much despite his humble beginnings. He had come to the shores of America as a penniless immigrant, with nothing but a burning desire to succeed. That desire ended up making him one of America's greatest success stories.

SUGGESTED READINGS

Joseph Frazier Wall's *Andrew Carnegie* [Oxford University Press, 1970] (University of Pittsburgh Press, 1989) is the most complete biography of Andrew Carnegie. George Swetnam's *Andrew Carnegie* (Boston: Twayne Publishers, 1980) is a study of his literary legacy. For a study in contrast between conservative and liberal interpretations, see, respectively, Louis M. Hacker, *The World of Andrew Carnegie, 1865–1901* (Philadelphia: J.B. Lippincott, 1968) and Robert Green McCloskey, *American Conservatism in the Age of Enterprise, 1865–1910* [1951] (New York: Harper & Row, 1964). Other recommendations include: Andrew Carnegie, *Autobiography* [Houghton Mifflin, 1920] (Boston: Northeastern University Press, 1986); Andrew Carnegie, *The Gospel of Wealth and Other Timely Essays,* ed. Edward C.

Kirkland (Cambridge: Belknap Press, 1962); and Burton W. Folsom, Jr., *The Myth of the Robber Barons: A New Look at the Rise of Big Business in America* [originally *Entrepreneurs vs. the State*, 1987] (3rd ed. Herndon, VA: Young America's Foundation, 1996).

INDEX

ABOUT THE
AUTHORS

George Roche has served as president of Hillsdale College since 1971. Formerly the presidential-appointed chairman of the National Council on Education Research, the director of seminars at the Foundation for Economic Education, a professor of history at the Colorado School of Mines, and a U.S. Marine, he is the author of twelve books, including, most recently, *The Fall of the Ivory Tower: Government Funding, Corruption, and the Bankrupting of American Higher Education* (Regnery, 1994). He received his Ph.D. in American history from the University of Colorado.

Since 1985, Lissa Roche has served as the director of seminars at Hillsdale College. She is also the managing editor of the college's monthly speech digest, *Imprimis*, and the Hillsdale College Press. In 1995, Crossway Books published her anthology, *The Christian's Treasury: Stories and Songs, Poems and Prayers, and Much More for Young and Old.* She has written articles and reviews for a wide variety of publications, including *Human Events,* the *Detroit News, USA Today* magazine, the *Orange Country Register,* and the *World and I.* She holds an M.A. in American history from the University of Notre Dame.